TEAM BUILDING
A practical guide for trainers

D0117593

Team Building

A practical guide for trainers

Neil Clark

The McGraw-Hill Companies

London · New York · St Louis · San Francisco · Auckland
Bogotá · Caracas · Lisbon · Madrid · Mexico · Milan
Montreal · New Delhi · Panama · Paris · San Juan · São Paulo
Singapore · Sydney · Tokyo · Toronto

Published by
McGRAW-HILL Book Company Europe
Shoppenhangers Road, Maidenhead, Berkshire, SL6 2QL, England.
Telephone 01628 23432
Fax 01628 770224

British Library Cataloguing in Publication Data
Clark, Neil
   Team Building: Practical Guide for
   Trainers.—(McGraw-Hill Training
   Series)
   I. Title   II. Series
   658.3

   ISBN 0-07-707846-2

Library of Congress Cataloging-in-Publication Data
Clark, Neil
     Team building: a practical guide for trainers / Neil Clark.
         p.   cm.—(McGraw-Hill training series)
     Includes bibliographical references and index.
     ISBN 0-07-707846-2
     1. Work groups—Handbooks, manuals, etc. I. Title.   II. Series.
   HD66.C497   1994   94-4259
   658.4'02—dc20   CIP

McGraw-Hill
A Division of The McGraw-Hill Companies

4 CUP 96

Typeset by BookEns Limited, Baldock, Herts
and printed and bound in Great Britain at the University Press, Cambridge
Printed on permanent paper in compliance with ISO Standard 9706

Contents

Series preface

Training and development are now firmly centre stage in most organizations, if not all. Nothing unusual in that—for some organizations. They have always seen training and development as part of the heart of their businesses—but more and more must see it that same way.

The demographic trends through the 1990s will inject into the marketplace severe competition for good people who will need good training. Young people without conventional qualifications, skilled workers in redundant crafts, people out of work, women wishing to return to work—all will require excellent training to fit them to meet the job demands of the 1990s and beyond.

But excellent training does not spring from what we have done well in the past. T&D specialists are in a new ball game. 'Maintenance' training—training to keep up skill levels to do what we have always done—will be less in demand. Rather, organization, work and market change training are now much more important and will remain so for some time. Changing organizations and people is no easy task, requiring special skills and expertise which, sadly, many T&D specialists do not possess.

To work as a 'change' specialist requires us to get to centre stage—to the heart of the company's business. This means we have to ask about future goals and strategies, and even be involved in their development, at least as far as T&D policies are concerned.

This demands excellent communication skills, political expertise, negotiating ability, diagnostic skills—indeed, all the skills a good internal consultant requires.

The implications for T&D specialists are considerable. It is not enough merely to be skilled in the basics of training, we must also begin to act like business people and to think in business terms and talk the language of business. We must be able to resource training not just from within but by using the vast array of external resources. We must be able to manage our activities as well as any other manager. We must share in the creation and communication of the company's vision. We must never let the goals of the company out of our sight.

In short, we may have to grow and change with the business. It will be hard. We shall not only have to demonstrate relevance but also value for money and achievement of results. We shall be our own boss, as accountable for results as any other line manager, and we shall have to deal with fewer internal resources.

The challenge is on, as many T&D specialists have demonstrated to me over the past few years. We need to be capable of meeting that challenge. This is why McGraw-Hill Book Company Europe have planned and launched this major new training series—to help us meet that challenge.

The series covers all aspects of T&D and provides the knowledge base from which we can develop plans to meet the challenge. They are practical books for the professional person. They are a starting point for planning our journey into the twenty first century.

Use them well. Don't just read them. Highlight key ideas, thoughts, action pointers or whatever, and have a go at doing something with them. Through experimentation we evolve; through stagnation we die.

I know that all the authors in the McGraw-Hill Training Series would want me to wish you good luck. Have a great journey into the twenty-first century.

ROGER BENNETT
Series Editor

About the series editor

Roger Bennett has over 20 years' experience in training, management education, research and consulting. He has long been involved with trainer training and trainer effectiveness. He has carried out research into trainer effectiveness, and conducted workshops, seminars, and conferences on the subject around the world. He has written extensively on the subject including the book *Improving Trainer Effectiveness* (Gower). His work has taken him all over the world and has involved directors of companies as well as managers and trainers.

Dr Bennett has worked in engineering, several business schools (including the International Management Centre, where he launched the UK's first master's degree in T&D), and has been a board director of two companies. He is the Editor of the *Journal of European Industrial Training* and was series editor of the ITD's *Get In There* workbook and video package for the managers of training departments. He now runs his own business called The Management Development Consultancy.

Preface

This is a book for trainers who want to know *how* to design and provide team building events. Therefore, the amount of theory on teams, team building and organization development is limited to the purely functional, i.e., what a trainer needs to provide this service. Readers with an interest in the academic aspects of these types of learning interventions already have a body of work available to them. (See Bibliography, p. 115).

The major impetus for writing this book has been the work that I have undertaken for HM Customs & Excise in the last few years. Although I have provided team building for other organizations in the same period (in total over 60 such events for 6 different organizations in the last 5 years), the particular demands placed on me as a consultant by HM Customs & Excise have encouraged me to reassess my views and practices. For me, this has proved to be a very good example of a collaborative learning process between a consultant and a client organization.

This period of assessment has been prompted by two particular factors. First, right from the start of my involvement with the Department, team building has been seen as one of the major vehicles for changing the culture of the organization towards the approach advocated in their publication 'Customs & Excise People'. (Among other things, this document advocates a more responsive and open form of management.) This has meant that the behavioural and attitudinal outcomes of team building have been of special interest to both facilitators and managers attending the events. Second, I have also designed and run training programmes for the internal management trainers to enable them to provide team building programmes within the Department. In providing programmes to meet their needs, I found that many of my 'intuitive' decisions about events actually arose from an evolving framework that is described in this book—a clear case of using theory to explain the practice. Therefore, I wish to acknowledge my thanks to HM Customs & Excise for the opportunity to work with them at both these levels. In particular, I wish to thank the Personnel Director, Dennis Battle, and the Assistant Secretary responsible for Training Services Division, May Smith.

I have not been alone on this journey. The internal trainer who has accompanied me every step of the way is Sid Perry, Training Services Division, whose contribution and support I gratefully appreciate. Fortunately, his modesty does not completely disguise his skills and talents as a trainer and consultant. We have worked effectively as a team and have contributed in turn to the wider team of facilitators working for the Department.

I would also like to take this opportunity to thank all those teams that have allowed me to work with them. I hope that I have always respected the invitation, however temporary, to be part of the team.

Finally, I am also grateful to the family team of my wife, Sylvia, and our children Simon, Iain and Jenny, who have provided the support and freedom necessary to produce this book.

Introduction

This book is aimed at the trainer working within, or for, an organization and providing programmes in management development or interpersonal skills. My expectations about your knowledge and experience are on the modest side and run to no more than you having provided, say, half a dozen programmes in these areas. From this you will have gained sufficient experience of standing in front of a group of managers and expecting them to examine, with a view to changing, their behaviours and/ or attitudes. Hopefully, whatever the subsequent longevity of your career as a trainer, the enormity of the demand that you place on delegates will never be allowed to dissipate from your awareness. Only if we regularly attend similar events as delegates ourselves are we able to safeguard against the possibility of taking personal learning for granted.

This book is laid out in a logical order, enabling you to come to terms with the issues and problems of team building in the order that they are likely to arise in practise. At each stage, the relevant theory, which will be kept to a minimum, will be described. However, it is really important that you do not rush into the chapters about designing events without reading the earlier chapters about the consultancy activity. The events should be seen as adjuncts to the consultancy, not the other way round.

This book has been written to be of interest, too, to the more experienced trainer who has, over the years, provided team building along with other training and development activities. In describing events or issues that you have experienced, I hope that I might be offering a different perspective to old problems. At worst, I hope that I may confirm that at least one other person has made a similar decision in the same circumstances. At best, what I hope that I offer you is an overall framework for identifying what I have referred to as *generic approaches* to team building. These different approaches, and their underlying rationale, are intended to offer a different perspective. I do not intend to offer a variation on the theme of '60 Team Building Activities'. I will include some activities, but these are merely to illustrate the approaches described and I wish to stress that the *context* of these activities is far more important than the activities alone. I hope that this book does more to stimulate your ideas and approaches than simply act as a source to cannibalize; I would hate to think I am providing a contribution to what I describe in Chapter 3 as the 'Allsorts Approach'.

At one level the market-place seems to be sated with books and manuals on team building. There would appear to be little new to say or offer. However, if you look in detail at the literature, what you will discover, apart from the activities-based books already mentioned, is that the rest are concerned with a 'brand name' approach to team building, albeit, Action Centred Leadership and the work of John Adair;[1] descriptions of outdoor training approaches; or instrumented approaches, e.g., the work of Dr R.M. Belbin.[2] What is missing is an overall framework for assessing the relevance of these different approaches for a particular team. This means that trainers have to rely on old, trusted favourites *irrespective of their relevance to the needs of a particular team*. What is also missing is a step-by-step guide for the trainer on how to *use* these different approaches, and a description of the choices and decisions that need to be made long before an event actually takes place.

To illustrate the nature of this problem, my own experience of becoming involved in team building is not untypical of what confronts most trainers. On being approached by a manager to run an event for his team, I merely asked him to identify the problems as he saw them, then used his list to compile a menu of topics for a programme. Although the event was well received, it was patently obvious to all of us that if the team *had* developed, it was purely accidental. The fact that they had experienced a happy event together was now part of their common history, contributing to that desired commodity, *esprit de corps*—the same kind of development that most learning groups should experience on any kind of event. Subsequent events with other teams were little better. As a more experienced trainer, I had discovered important resources, such as Pfeiffer and Jones,[3] and had also learned to steal activities from my colleagues. This ability to 'borrow' material—to the great grief of authors and publishers—is one of the survival skills of every trainer. By exercising this skill, therefore, the content of my team building programmes became more interesting and creative, at least to me as facilitator. This improvement, in content and style, did not disguise, alas, the inability of these events to address the needs of a particular team.

The next stage in the evolution of my approach to team building was the nirvana of unstructured training. The premise with this approach is that the team, by learning to cope with the uncertainty that you inflict on them will, *faut de mieux*, discover the skills and knowledge required to improve their performance as a team. At a superficial level, there is a convincing attraction in this argument. At a more practical level, there are some fairly obvious problems with it. The first is that teams which did discover how to fill the vacuum of uncertainty created by the trainer found it difficult to transfer these skills to the workplace. The skills of being open, asking for what you want, expressing feelings, giving feed-back and so on—all important skills for any team—do not improve the performance of a team when they arise in isolation and have no context. Their use during the event develops an open climate for that period of time, but they also need to be rooted in the normal practice of the team to have a lasting beneficial effect. Similarly, the identification of personal attributes, behaviours or roles, however interesting, do not develop the knowledge, skills and attitudes required for effective team working. These learning points need to be founded in a work, not a training, context.

What I have learned as a trainer is that structure and guidance are the prerequisites for organizational learning. In the area of team building the 'how' of this is a point that has not been seriously addressed. It is what I have attempted to do in this book.

Where possible, I have eschewed the theoretical in favour of the practical. My concern is to focus on the question 'What do I (the trainer) do next?' Having offered an answer, I then address the question 'Why do it that way?' In following this approach, I have deliberately dodged many of the issues beloved by behavioural scientists. For example, how to define a team, the appropriate size of an effective team, and differences in types of teams. My experiences as both trainer and consultant have taught me that managers who request team building seem remarkably untroubled by the niceties of definition. For them, membership of a particular team is self-evident, i.e., they all report to the same manager, and they are regularly invited to meetings the purposes of which include one or more of the following: to share information, solve problems and/ or make decisions. Similarly, without being able to define what team building is, they are tremendously articulate about the problems that they want it to resolve, e.g., to improve the quality and commitment to decision making, improve communication, resolve interpersonal problems and so on.

I hope that I take a similar pragmatic approach in both the structure and content of this book. Therefore, I start from the first point of contact between the team leader and the trainer. This is because what the last 20 years have demonstrated to me is that the team building event is merely one step in a vital consultancy activity, and not necessarily the most important step either. As I demonstrated in my account of my first experience of team building training described above, my initial response to the team leader involved me taking a trainer role, i.e., responding to the 'felt' training needs that he identified. Since then, I have come to appreciate that such a request needs a consultant, not a trainer, response. Team building should be seen as a consultancy activity, not a training event. Purists might argue that training should also be a consultancy activity, but, in the real world, such things are arranged differently; the systematic approach to training is more honoured in the breach than the observance. The role of the consultant makes different demands than that of the trainer and these need to be understood by those who wish to develop in this direction. Therefore, Chapter 1, is concerned with setting team building in the context of the consultancy relationship with the client and looking at the particular demands this makes on the internal trainer.

Chapter 2 deals with the next step in the activity, i.e., early interventions with the team, including the option of Process Consultancy. Having established this wider context, Chapter 3 examines some examples of existing 'brand name' approaches to team building. Based on this review, it is stated that the need for team building has to be rooted in an established and accepted view of what is an effective team. This view should provide both a diagnostic tool with which the problems faced by a particular team can be identified and should also offer, albeit implicitly, clear learning aims, in terms of knowledge, skill and attitude, for addressing these problems. Equally important, for my needs, is that this view should not be tied to one particular approach to team building. It should be able to embrace, and add to, the existing 'brand name' approaches. This view, which I shall describe at length in this chapter, is derived from the work of Edgar Schein.[4] After describing some of his key concepts, I identify what I call three *generic approaches* to team building.

Chapters 4 to 6 will contain descriptions of these generic approaches to team building with examples of structures for the programmes and typical activities that can be offered. Each of these chapters will talk about the relevance of the approach to different kinds of teams, methodology and design features of such programmes, the kinds of problems likely to arise, and guidance for the trainer on how to deal with them.

Finally, in Chapter 7, I look at the wider context of the organization and how this can influence both the team and the trainer. I will also offer some ideas on how team building can and, in my judgement, should, be seen as part of an overall strategy to change, develop, or reinforce a particular culture. In simple terms, such a strategy would aim to develop the whole organization as one, integrated, functioning team. As part of this strategy, I will be addressing such issues as managing relationships between teams, developing the manager to undertake team building and examining some of the problems faced by the internal trainer when taking on this role.

When I started my career in training 20 years ago, my involvement in team building was fairly episodic—consisting of, at most, two or three events in a year. By contrast, in the last five years I have been averaging about ten events each year. The increased demand for this kind of intervention is symptomatic of a need on the part of organizations to be more responsive to the increased demands placed on them by the environments in which they operate. Having recognized this need, a number of organizations are implementing strategies based on team building that seek to develop the appropriate skills and attitudes to manage change more effectively.

References

1 Adair, John, *Effective Teambuilding*. Gower, 1986.
2 Belbin, Dr R.M. *Management Teams: Why They Succeed or Fail*. Heinemann, 1981.
3 Pfeiffer, J. William, and Jones, John E., *A Handbook of Structured Experiences*, 10 vols., University Associates, 1974–83.
4 Schein, Edgar, *Process Consultation* (2nd ed.), 2 vols. Addison-Wesley, 1988.

1 The client relationship

Introduction Team building can be simply defined as a structured attempt to improve/develop the effectiveness of a group of people who work (temporarily or permanently) together. This improvement/development may be particularly focused in terms of outputs, e.g., the speed and quality of decisions and actions produced by the team, or in terms of more nebulous areas, e.g., the quality of relationships, greater cooperation, more of a corporate attitude. What most approaches aim to develop in behavioural terms can be summarized as shown in Figure 1.1.

Reticent	Communicative
Secretive and reserved	Open
Conflict	Cooperation
Apprehensive	Trusting
Impersonal	Mutual concern
Avoidance of responsibility	Self-responsibility
Sterility	Creativity
Alienation	Commitment
Role confusion	Role clarity
Individual-centred	Team-centred

Figure 1.1 *Behavioural aims of team building*

Many organizations still appear to operate on the assumption that the act of promotion, plus the minimum of management training, are enough to equip managers with the skills to be both effective leaders and members of teams. By virtue of bringing together a group of managers, either as the normal product of the organization hierarchy or as members selected to carry out a project, then, it is expected, they will work effectively together as a team. Part of the assumption that underpins this view is a basic belief in people being reasonable and cooperative. Therefore, when it has to be acknowledged that a team is *not* working effectively, the habitual response of both team members and others is to view the situation as being caused by deviant behaviour or the unfortunate product of a personality clash. Either way, effective team working is looked on as being both desirable and the norm in most organizations. At the same time, ineffective team working is seen as an aberration—in need of a cure. Unfortunately, these assumptions do not really bear inspection. Anyone privileged to observe work teams in action will quickly come to the conclusion that effective teams are rarely found. The majority of teams are handicapped by different degrees of ineffectiveness. Observers will also discover that there appears to be little direct correlation between experience, seniority and effective team working. If anything, there may be an inverse correlation. That is to say, the more experienced and senior the membership, the more bad habits of team working they have developed over time.

Teams exist within an environment that still appears to reward insularity, competitiveness, manipulation and dishonesty. Although there appears to be a healthy recognition that these attitudes and behaviours need to change, we have created generations of managers who have been rewarded for exactly these traditional attributes. They are unlikely to willingly surrender what they have learned and been rewarded for exhibiting. Nor have we provided appropriate training to develop effective team working, particularly at a senior level. Despite these factors, for many managers, team building is seen as a remedial rather than a development activity. This view breeds resentment, which is likely to be exacerbated by conditions of resource shortage and an increasing need to be more competitive. The daily grind of 'getting the job done' appears to be a very good reason for avoiding the perceived luxury (or indulgence) of team building. Despite the obvious *need* for team building in most organizations, then, there is often well-established resistance to the prospect.

Because of these resistances, and the behaviours and attitudes that are barely concealed by the resistances, the trainer needs to approach team building with informed caution. There are particular aspects of team building that make the activity distinctly different from any other training event he or she may have experienced.

Differences between team building and training

1 The team has a history and their current behaviour and attitudes are the product of months, sometimes years, of interaction. This history may not be known by all the members, but it retains a power and influence on the present and helps to explain why certain things happen. For example, we, the older members, know that Jane and Bill have sniped at each other since that meeting two years ago when Bill stormed out. The new member is only aware of the frosty relationship between them.

2 The team has a future. Whatever takes place on the event, the one probability is that this team will need to continue to work together. To ensure that this is possible, the team will be more than willing to act 'irrationally'—to collude in denial, or avoidance, of major problems affecting the team's performance. For example, they will choose to treat as a fact of life a particular subgroup of members who resist all forms of change on principle. In doing so, the rest of the team end up supporting the resistance that they will also decry.

3 The team needs to be looked on as a complicated organism that has achieved its primary objective, i.e., to survive. In the process of achieving this aim, individuals have learned to make trade-offs regarding their needs. They have also learned how to reward and punish appropriate behaviours within the team. Often, when talking about themselves, members will naturally reach for sporting metaphors to illustrate some aspect of their behaviour. A more appropriate analogy for me is that of a family—the layers of complexity, the codes, rituals and so on that are so obvious to the family member are often totally opaque to the outsider. The process of competition in teams seems more like sibling rivalry than open, sporting competition.

4 The team has a definable role and purpose and is clearly accountable to one person in the organization. That person is likely to have particular expectations of its future performance. (Although these factors apply to a training group, the roles, purposes and accountability are so diffuse as to have little bearing on the learning event.)

5 If a team member is likely to experience a conflict of loyalties about whose side to take on an issue, he or she will be likely to choose that of a colleague in preference to that of a trainer.

I raise these differences early and in stark terms, because the trainer needs every encouragement *not* to put on the trainer's hat. The risk levels for both trainer and group are much higher than are likely to be experienced on even the most unstructured forms of training. All the above issues can be avoided by simply running a standard training programme for a team or making the event so anodyne that there is little chance of anything happening. What ensues from such a choice may be described as many things but team building is certainly not it.

The trainer as consultant

In terms of avoiding these pitfalls, the first skill that needs to be developed by the trainer is that of saying, 'No'. The habitual response of the internal trainer is to say 'Yes' to any request, even when it is against their better judgement. Team building is not always appropriate for all teams and may not be the answer to the particular problem being posed by the manager in the role of client. In a similar vein, the trainer should avoid 'selling' team building to a manager or a team. Offering information about team building, including the problems and pitfalls is a better service for all concerned.

In my experience, the request for a particular event can come from a variety of sources and may not be from either the team leader or a team member. A senior manager may prescribe, at a distance, the need for this particular team to be developed, or a local trainer may suggest that there might be benefits to gain from undertaking such a venture. Wherever the request originates from, the trainer should view this as the first point of contact between themselves and a potential client, that is to say, the first stage in the process of consultation.

I have described elsewhere[1] an approach to the process of consultation. For convenience, I will limit myself here to describing briefly some of the key stages and the kinds of issues that need to be dealt with at each stage. The particular stages that I wish to pay attention to in this and the next chapter are:

- gaining entry
- analysis
- diagnosis
- implementation.

Gaining entry

The request for team building having been made, it is important for the trainer to recognize that, whoever originated the suggestion, the team leader can be the only *client* for a team building programme. Others may have a view about the efficacy or otherwise of this kind of intervention, but, ultimately, the trainer needs to disregard their views. Dealing with these other parties may be difficult to manage, particularly when the person expressing that view is a very senior member of the organization. Under such circumstances, many team leaders are inclined to go along with the suggestions offered. For the same reason, the internal trainer will have a similar inclination. Their willingness to follow the advice, unfortunately, is not good enough. A trainer who enters into a consultancy relationship with a passive client, i.e., someone willing to give it a try, has begun to take too much responsibility for the learning and the team. The danger of working under these circumstances is that the trainer becomes the *de facto* team leader while the real one abdicates their responsibility for the effective management of the team.

For the same reason, I, as a trainer, will never attempt to 'sell' the virtues of team building to a client. Where appropriate, I will choose, instead, to describe what happens on a team building event and, also, what the problems or difficulties can be. Only once having offered this information will I then choose to talk about the potential benefits. The reason for such caution is that it is very easy, and, to some extent, understandable, for management responsibilities to be assumed by the trainer. First, most team leaders start out the consultancy relationship being dependant on the knowledge and skills of the trainer. Second, most trainers have a tendency to want to take on too much responsibility for the learning of others (this is an occupational hazard).

It is very important, not least for the above reasons, that once the trainer does make contact with the client, that they resist rushing into talking about the team. What needs to be dealt with first is establishing the right relationship with the client. In particular, the trainer needs to find out the answers to some crucial questions. For example:

- What does the team leader want from this exercise?
- What does the team leader want from the trainer?
- What responsibility for the event is the team leader willing to take?

It is not unknown, in my experience, for a team leader to have a secondary agenda, which may or may not be hidden from the trainer. For example, that they want to offer one member of the team a last chance to change their behaviour or attitude, and this event is that opportunity, or, they want confirmation from others that another member of the team is not really capable of doing their job, or, want to prove to their own satisfaction that the 'problems' in the team are someone else's fault, or, want a 'failed' team building activity in order to give themselves permission to adopt a totally directive and non-consultative management style. In my experience, there is nothing sinister or wrong about these agendas, provided that the client is willing to talk about them with the trainer. In fact the declaration of such agendas in the first meeting with the client provides a very good basis for a working relationship. However, where these agendas remain both undisclosed and undetected by the trainer, serious trouble is bound to arise. This is because when these agendas are subsequently 'discovered' on the team building event, the prime casualty is trust. (This may occur in the relationship between the trainer and the client, and/or between the team and the client or trainer.) For this reason, in my early meetings with the client, if I have any suspicion about the client's motivation, I will confront them about it. The biggest risk I face in doing so is that my suspicions are correct and the team leader denies them and abhorts the activity—a decision that prevents a lot of potential hostility, suspicion and suffering.

At this stage, one firm clue that the client's expectations for the event are realistic is that they will describe themselves as an integral part of the team. For example, the leader will talk about 'our' strengths and weaknesses. They will accept personal responsibility for both their actions and their consequences. There will be no blaming of others: their general approach will be to want to include all members.

I will then ask what they want from me as a trainer. To help them answer this question, I will describe in some detail the options available for running the event and I will outline the likely consequences of working at the task, group or individual levels. (These approaches will be described in detail in Chapters 4 to 6.) I will also tell them what I am willing to offer as part of the relationship, e.g.:

- information derived from interviews (without breaching confidentiality)
- my perceptions of individuals and the team
- feedback
- counselling.

I will also tell them what I want from them as a client:

- feedback to me
- their honest views about individuals in the team
- their continued and overt support for agreed action during the consultancy
- their advice on how to progress the activity.

Typically, the kind of requests that are made of me by team leaders are to have regular contact to discuss progress, a request for honest feedback and an opportunity to talk thorough their perceptions and concerns about the team. The more explicit this process of contract setting, the greater the probability of effective team building. I say to my clients, in this first interview, that the team building process actually starts with this meeting, not least because the quality of the relationship that the trainer establishes with the client is usually a reliable guide to the quality of relationships within the team. For example, if you come away from your meeting with the client feeling uncertain or unclear, there is a great possibility that this will also be a characteristic of relationships within the team.

At this stage, one important piece of information will not be available to the trainer. This piece of information is the actual behaviour that takes place between the leader and the team. Sometimes the gap between the way a leader talks about their relationships with individuals and their *actual* behaviour with them can be quite dramatic. For example, they may talk in a very neutral and objective way about a particular individual, but their actual behaviour with this person is characterized by tense and jokey small talk. How willing a particular team leader is to acknowledge their difficulties in dealing with certain members of their team will vary, depending on the clarity of their self-awareness and their willingness to avoid pretending that, as leader, they have to be infallible. The overwhelming majority of leaders that I have worked with have been able, after the first interview, to let these barriers down and willingly talk about their difficult relationships within the team.

In any team building event, the team leader is always likely to be the most vulnerable member. First, because the appropriateness or otherwise of their management style is likely to be a key factor for review. Second, because everyone else in the team is likely to be in an authority relationship with the leader. Third, because there appears to be a learned pattern of behaviour in teams that if a problem does exist, the leader is primarily culpable for not having dealt with the cause. For these reasons, the leader will require a lot of support from the trainer. The leader's awareness of their own potential vulnerability and the way they deal with the prospect of this situation is an important area that the trainer needs to pay attention to. If the leader shows a macho response to the prospect of being vulnerable or minimizes this problem, the trainer needs to tread carefully for it is likely that the leader will manifest similar kinds of defensive behaviour on the event and this is likely to have a detrimental effect on team members. In response to such an attitude, they are likely to act tough just to elicit a response from the leader or, more likely, they are going to enter the event suitably armoured to protect themselves from a defensive leader. The major casualties of such attitudes will obviously be openness and honesty. There will also be a terminal inability to develop support as part of the team's culture. What will be fostered, instead, is the John Wayne attitude, 'You have to be tough to survive'. The leader's need to be tough will be reciprocated by the team and so this aspect of their culture will be reinforced.

My advice to all potential team builders is that it you have any doubts about the team leader and your relationship with them, then do not go ahead with an event. It is unlikely that a questionable relationship will come 'all right on the night'. In reality, an uncertain relationship is likely to take a dramatic turn for the worse. Such a gap between client and trainer can be quickly filled with suspicion when the pressure is on. For any kind of team building event to be effective, the client and the trainer have to be in a partnership of equality and mutual interdependence. From the trainer's side, the responsibility should be to help the client and the team to manage their relationship effectively. From the client's side, the responsibility is to help the trainer assist the team to learn to manage itself more effectively.

Assuming that the first meeting has been successful, the trainer needs to agree a contract to undertake some form of analysis and diagnosis. This will involve the trainer subsequently returning to the leader with a recommendation about the appropriateness of an intervention that might, or might not, include team building. It is worth alerting the leader that the process of analysis (the various choices will be described below) will have an impact on how the team currently operates. This influence can often lead to some fairly dramatic, though essentially short-term, changes of behaviour. Quite often, team members will develop a sudden rash of cooperative and helpful behaviours with each other. They may even joke openly about what they are doing by being so helpful. In extreme cases, individuals may get together to collude in presenting an image or view about the team's performance, e.g., we have no problems. Often, and not surprisingly, the prospect of team building is looked on as a threat or as some form of critical judgement about their ability. This perception can develop into resistance or denial. The choice of analysis needs to be strong enough to counter this possibility. Ideally, the choice of analysis should also provide an opportunity for the trainer to have a positive influence on this resistance. (I will come back to the wider issue of resistance and how to manage it later in this chapter.)

Analysis

The purpose of analysis is to gain information about how the team functions and there are three different types of information available. The first type I would label *hard information*. This invariably describes what *should* happen and most of it is usually available in written form. This would include:

- organization structure
- agendas for meetings
- minutes of meetings
- procedural documents

- statistics
- technical manuals
- policy statements
- job descriptions, etc., etc.

One other characteristic of this type of information is that it purports to be objective, although I suspect that many readers are well aware of the ability of minutes to portray an imaginative, rather than truthful, account of events. Similarly, all the other above sources can be nearer to fiction than truth. At the first meeting, many team leaders will have this kind of information to hand and believe it to be a valuable source for the trainer. In practical terms, it can often seduce the trainer into unimportant content issues at the expense of being able to see the wider picture of the environment in which the team operates.

The second source available can, by contrast, be labelled *soft information*. The important quality of this information is that it is highly subjective. It includes:

- opinions
- perceptions
- feelings
- behaviour
- relationships
- observations.

The particular characteristic of this information is that it should tell you what *actually* happens. The simple gap between what *should* and what *does* happen is often a reliable gauge of the issues that need to be worked on.

The third area for analysis is *history*. This should comprise a mixture of both hard and soft information and is unlikely to be in written form. Interestingly, the variations in a team's history not only embrace wide differences on the *reasons* for events, but also include glaring discrepancies in the *recall* of the events themselves. Often, the public sharing of these perceptions is a major event on a team building programme, when an individual realizes that an accepted fact is actually a myth.

In terms of gathering the information, the trainer can use one or more of three different approaches:

- questionnaires
- interviews
- observations.

Questionnaires A number of standard team effectiveness questionnaires are available for use.[2] My own experiences of using questionnaires for analysis is that their primary function is not the production of information, but that of stimulating members to think about the way the team functions. For this reason, I tend to use an example like that in Figure 1.2.

In order to help me to understand how this team works I would like your cooperation in answering the following questions. Please do not attempt to be too analytical as I am interested in your initial responses to these areas:

1 How satisfied are you by your contribution at meetings?

2 How would you describe the way this team makes decisions?

3 How well does this team solve problems?

4 How effectively do team members work together?

5 How effectively does the leader manage meetings?

6 What could be done to improve the effectiveness of meetings?

7 What could you do to make this team more effective?

Figure 1.2   *Team effectiveness questionnaire*

When using questionnaires, it is advisable to do so only after talking directly to members of the team about the purpose of the analysis and to offer unequivocal guarantees about the confidentiality of the information they are being asked to provide. I am very reluctant to use questionnaires as the sole means of analysis, largely because they are a limited, one-way method of communication that raise more questions, in my experience, than answers. They also arouse an expectation among team members that the trainer is committed to using this information in some 'expert' way, i.e., it will lead to a recommendation for action. If not, they think, why have I been asked to complete this document? However, as an adjunct to other forms of analysis, they can be useful for providing a snapshot of where the team is now.

Interviews   My single, preferred method of analysis is one-to-one interviews with members of the team. The reasons for this are not just to do with the improved quality of information received, but that they provide an opportunity for the trainer to develop a relationship with each team member. Although it would not be possible, or even desirable, to aim for the same kind of relationship as with the leader, each team member is likely to have concerns about, and needs to be met by the trainer. Their needs are likely to include:

- information about team building
- assurances about the nature of what will take place
- clarification of the role of the trainer
- guidelines about the information that they are giving.

In addition to these basic needs, they will also be looking, explicitly or implicitly, for some key information about the trainer. In addition to wanting to know about his or her qualifications and experience in this area, they will need to find ways to reassure themselves that the trainer is trustworthy and supportive at a personal level. Quite simply, they will want to know to what extent the trainer is impartial and equable. In order to make this need easier to fulfil, I start each interview by offering information. Typically, I would explain:

- the purpose of the interview (to give me information to help me reach a judgement about the appropriateness of team building)
- that I will be reporting back to the leader a summary of the information that is presented to me, but without breaching individual confidentiality
- the kind of event that is being proposed, what will take place *and what will be expected of them* (including any preparatory work)
- background information about the request for team building
- information about my professional work in team building.

Having checked with the person whether or not they have received enough information, I ask them to tell me, in this sequence, their personal experience of membership, their perceptions of each member of the team and their views about the proposed team building programme. I would normally allow about 90 minutes for each interview and ask their permission to make written notes of their answers. Again, I reassure them that the notes are for my use only. Ideally, these interviews should take place about four weeks before the proposed event. In my experience, this provides the optimum balance between the needs for preparation, without there being the danger that the event seems a long way off, and can therefore be dropped to the back of the attention of the team members.

In many ways, the content of these interviews—what is actually said—is less important than the *way* in which it is said. The way the person tells their 'story' is usually a fairly reliable guide to their behaviour as a team member. For example, the person who volunteers their views in a grudging fashion and with caution, is likely to have a similar style in meetings. My continuing experience is that the overwhelming majority of people tell the 'truth' as they perceive it and no attempt is made to lie in these interviews. There is an obvious safeguard for detecting such a possibility—the consensual view that begins to emerge from the rest of the interviews. A 'deviant' or 'individualistic' view stands out from the body of opinion that emerges over time. What, in my experience, produces this version of events is not so much deliberate falsehood as a very poorly developed sense of awareness. Sometimes, this can be dramatically apparent, e.g., when a team member's perception of their colleagues is invariably coloured by a suspicion of their motivation. For such a person, everyone has a hidden agenda—apart from themselves. At other times, this poverty of perception is less obvious. One safeguard I build into the interviews is to conclude by asking the speaker to tell me how they imagine their colleagues would describe them to me. If there is a major divergence between their awareness of themselves and what I know their colleagues have said, then a fairly independent source for judgement is my experience of the speaker. If I have doubts about the quality of their perceptions, I will offer the speaker some feedback *based on my experiences of them*. Sometimes my feedback is descriptive, e.g., 'I notice that you speak very fast and do not look at me', but, most times under these circumstances, my feedback would be interpretative, e.g., 'My guess is that you would be a difficult person to ask for help. My concern about doing so is that you would look down on me for asking.' What I am wanting to check is not the accuracy, or otherwise, of my feedback, but how the person responds. Do they, for example, instinctively reject or accept the feedback? Do they seek to explain or 'attempt to help me understand'? Do they think about the content, then make a clear statement about what makes sense to them about what I have said.

In addition to allowing them to make judgements about me as a trainer, I am also making judgements about them as members on a team building programme. In positive terms, I am looking for a person who will approach such an activity with the intention to both contribute and be open to learning and influence. (Like all other trainers I accept, wearily, my share of those individuals who are willing to approach the event with 'an open mind'.) I am also looking for evidence of some contraindicators. Some of the more obvious negatives clues would be:

- expression of very emotional concerns about a proposed team build-ing programme, e.g., 'I think we will be involved in bloodletting'
- continuing agitation and an inability to focus on one topic of conver-sation
- a desire to speed up the interview to a quick closure
- paranoia that feeds off new information instead of being dissipated during the interview
- evidence of spite and continual blaming of others for any, and all, misfortunes
- unending expressions of disbelief about the value of such an event, concluded by a statement that the speaker holds out a faint hope of being converted.

When I experience any of the above, I confront the speaker with my concerns and what I believe may be the consequences of their behaviour on the event. If my doubts are confirmed, I tell the speaker that, should the event take place, then my recommendation to their manager will be that they do not attend. (For the reasoning behind this recommendation and the practical consequences that flow from it, see Resistance, Chapter 2.)

The majority of people attending such events do have genuine concerns that can be dealt with quite adequately at the interview stage. Commonly, these concerns embrace the following areas:

- 'What is expected of me?' (i.e., 'What will I have to do?)
- 'What are the limits?' (e.g., 'How personal will we be?')
- 'Who is in charge and how will the event be policed?'
- 'What will be the practical outcomes of the activity?'
- 'What guarantees are available that my contribution to such an event will not be held against me in the future?'
- 'What happens if?' (This is usually a worst fantasy and is regularly expressed in terms of an unspecified member of the team being unable to cope. Invariably, it is the speaker who is the unspecified member.)

Unfortunately, the assurances offered to deal with these and similar concerns have an expiry date that comes into effect at the start of each team building programme. Therefore, whatever approach to team building is used, it is highly recommended that the first activity on any event will be the setting of ground rules. The purpose of these ground rules is to provide answers to the above questions (for examples of what might be included see under the appropriate section for the three main approaches).

It is not uncommon to find that the start of these interviews is marked by some degree of hostility and suspicion that, by the end, has mellowed to a genuine interest in the proposed event. However, in three or four weeks' time, at the start of the event, many individuals have reverted to their original levels of hostility and suspicion. The reasons for this reversion are that team members have taken the opportunity to talk about their interviews with the trainer. They have also had time to reflect on what they said at the interview and to speculate about what their colleagues might have said about them. The immediate result of these reflections and discussions is that the team have begun to coalesce around the discovery of a common enemy, that is, the trainer, and the fear of a prospective battlefield—the team building event.

Observations

The third form of analysis is to observe the team, or members of the team, in their daily tasks. The absolute minimum of time available for this will be that spent in the interviews themselves. Invariably the interviews will be taking place on their territory. The effectiveness, or otherwise, of the arrangements made will offer some important clues about the team. For example, were the interview times imposed on team members or were they consulted? Did someone take responsibility for hosting the trainer during this time or were they left on their own? Did team members turn up on time or were there unexplained delays or cancellations? To what extent had the team discussed the prospect of team building among themselves? Were they consulted or had the event been imposed? To what extent was the trainer made to feel welcome as opposed to being merely tolerated?

Similarly, important information can be gleaned from noticing how the team are physically located. Are they on separate floors? Are they located in individual offices and, if so, to what extent is it easy for another member of the team to enter? What is the pattern of social contact between members when the trainer moves from one interview to another? Are they friendly and chatty or dispassionate and formal? Is there any evidence available about their social contact with each other? For example, is there a common refreshment room? Do some, or all, go for lunches together? What kind of contact, if any, do they have outside work? One particular team that I worked with in Northern Ireland had all gone to school together, were still involved in a complicated pattern of sporting and social groups and all but one had asked for early retirement at the same time. This kind of information provides a very good guideline for the kind of risk level that the team will be prepared to tolerate.

In addition, the trainer can ask for the opportunity to attend a normal meeting of the team. This is a particularly valuable option for the trainer new to team building. They can not only gain some useful information, but can also take the opportunity to practise at a lower risk level a particular form of team building that Schein has described as *Process Consultancy*. (Process consultancy is described further at the beginning of the next chapter.)

Summary

In this chapter, I have offered a brief description of team building and have identified some important ways in which it differs from training. I have suggested that the trainer should see team building emerging from a consultancy relationship with the client—the team leader. I have then described some important steps in this relationship, from the point of first contact with the client to the completion of an analysis. In the next chapter, I will complete the next stage—establishing the right kind of intervention for the team.

References

1 Clark, Neil, *Managing personal learning and change*. McGraw-Hill, 1990.
2 Pfeiffer, J. William, (ed.) *The encyclopedia of team-building activities*, 2 vols, San Diego: Pfeiffer & Company, 1991. (See pp. 229–278 for some characteristic examples of questionnaires available.)

2 Understanding the team

Process Consultantancy

Edgar Schein[1] has defined Process Consultancy as 'a set of activities on the part of the consultant that help the client to perceive, understand, and act upon the process events that occur in the client's environment'.

In the context of team building, this involves the trainer observing the behaviour of individuals and the patterns of communication between them. By paying attention to the process (i.e., how the team work together), the trainer can, and should, disregard much of the content (i.e., what is said). The purpose of the observation is to provide the team with the information, and a structure, to undertake its own analysis and diagnosis. In considering this role, the trainer would be advised that the normal, non-directive role that they might use on a training programme is not a good choice for this activity. My experience of trainers who sit and observe a team for, say, two hours, and then proceed to start a review with a typical non-directive intervention like, 'I would be interested to hear your views about how the meeting went', would be swiftly rejected or punished in some way. If a team have asked you to observe them in action, they will be extremely frustrated if you do not offer some information.

To offset this danger, at the start of the meeting I tell the team what I am observing (see below) and how I will be offering my observations (i.e., as information for them to use). I will also agree with them an agreed time, say, 30 minutes, for the process review. When observing the process, the trainer has a choice about the kind of feedback to use:

- *descriptive* describing the observed behaviours, e.g., 'I saw X interrupt Y at 3.10', and these behaviours can be quantified, e.g., 'I saw X interrupt others 25 times'
- *interpretative* attempting to offer reasons for particular behaviours, e.g., 'You looked really upset at that stage and I wasn't surprised when you interrupted Y'.

Both kinds of feedback are valid, but, in general terms, descriptive feedback is a lower-risk choice for both giver and receiver.

The areas of process that are worth concentrating on are:

- communication
- structure of the meeting
- leadership

- decision-making process
- problem solving.

To aid me in this activity I just take a blank sheet with these headings and then make notes about what I find interesting in these areas. Particular aspects to look for in the various areas are as follows.

Communication Any obvious differences in the levels of contribution by individuals to discussions. Do the levels seem to relate to status, experience or other factors?

Any patterns of who talks to whom? One simple method for producing this information is to make a sociogram, which involves plotting the frequency and direction of comments made.

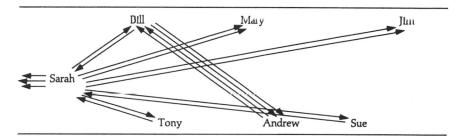

Figure 2.1   *Example of a sociogram*

Figure 2.1 represents what happens in the ten-minute sequence. The arrows represent the directions of the comments. The arrows that are not directed at a particular individual are overhead comments, e.g., 'Has everyone agreed to the proposal?'

What this particular sociogram shows is that Sarah, the leader, is tightly structuring the communication, e.g., most of the arrows are going to and from her. The only break from this pattern is the cross-talk between Bill and Andrew. In addition, Jim has been totally uninvolved in the discussion, while many of Mary's comments are addressed to the whole group. The fact that no arrows are coming back is likely to mean that her contributions have been lost.

Structure How is the meeting structured? Are there an agenda and minutes? Are agenda items labelled as to purpose (e.g., information, problem solving or decision making)? Are times allocated for different items? What is the overall length of the meeting? Who manages timekeeping and the conduct of members? Is management left entirely to the leader or do team members discipline themselves and each other? One good clue to the discipline of meetings is to watch what happens under 'any other business'. Members jostling to introduce a number of items or seeking to reopen issues discussed at the meeting are often clear indicators of underlying dissatisfaction. Similarly, look out for evidence of an overdisciplined approach, where contributions are brief to the point of curtness and there is an absence of different points of view.

Many managers, in my experience, are consciously trying to move away from old patterns of autocracy and have overreacted by offering no direction or structure. Instead, team members are encouraged to talk at length in the vain hope that this process will produce agreement. What it actually produces are meetings of marathon length and immense frustration.

Leadership

The style adopted by the leader will have a major impact on the performance of the team. The pattern of communication and the structure of the meeting will offer strong clues as to the nature of the style. It is worth watching how the leader introduces items for either discussion or problem solving. Do they clearly label what they want from their colleagues? To what extent do they exercise influence on the task (influencing the decision, solution or future action) and to what extent the process? If the latter, they will make little contribution about the matter in hand. Instead, they will be clarifying and summarizing the contributions of others. They will be managing the levels of contributions by individuals—bringing some people in and closing down others. Leaders who are driven by the task are likely to be unaware of these issues.

Watch also how the leader closes down discussions. Is there an attempt to summarize what others have said? If so, does the summary bear any relation to what went before? How are decisions called for? ('Does everyone agree?', is much more inviting than, 'Does anyone disagree?')

However you might describe the style, one of the key areas of concern is how individual members respond to the leader. What appears to be their level of satisfaction with the meeting? Watch for the operation of subgroups, 'personality clashes' and deviant individuals. These behaviours are likely to offer strong clues to underlying dissatisfactions and their perceived source. It is important to watch the non-verbal behaviours, particularly for examples of repressed contributions and unexpressed dissatisfactions.

Decision making

The number of decisions taken at meetings—even ostensible briefing meetings—are many and varied. What is interesting is the way in which each one is made. Some of the methods include:

- one individual making a proposal *that no one actually responds to*, but which becomes a decision binding on the team
- one person agreeing to a proposal made by another member that then becomes binding on the team
- the leader offering a point of view and asking, 'Are there any dissenters?'
- the leader summarizing after a discussion and offering the majority or consensus view that owes its origins to neither
- straight voting process involving counting heads
- the compromise solution that pleases some members
- genuine exploration of different points of view to seek an answer that satisfies everyone
- the decision enshrined in a history that only one or two people can actually recall.

More than the details of a particular decision, what appears to cause the most dissatisfaction in groups, is the lack of understanding and agreement about the *process* of decision making. Many teams have the tendency to force themselves into a belief that only two extremes of decision making are available—democracy or autocracy. It is interesting to clarify the meaning of these terms for individuals. For many people, the term 'democracy' is defined by the possibility of them winning, while 'autocracy' describes the prospect of them losing! Such teams then logically conclude that *both* options create problems!

Problem solving The approach that many teams take to problem solving is to limit the options as soon as possible and then find problems and difficulties in the few choices that they *do* consider. Little attention is paid to the generation of choices and, although the term 'brainstorming' is invariably used by teams, it actually describes only the tentative offering of ideas. What actually emerges from such discussions is little in the way of creativity, but, instead, a great deal of incremental problem solving, that is, like last time, but slightly different. Some of the patterns of contributions that help to paralyse attempts at problem solving are listed in Figure 2.2.

With all due respect . . .

Yes . . . but . . .

I hear what you say . . .

What you don't understand is . . .

I cannot say this often enough . . .

Everyone knows that . . .

It could not possibly . . .

It has been tried before . . .

I've listened to you long enough . . .

Figure 2.2 Group discussion blocks

Simply listing examples of these, and their variations, provides a lot of information for teams about the source of their frustration.

Using the information gained By offering feedback to groups, both descriptive and interpretative, in these five areas, teams are able to reach decisions both about their need for, and the particular nature of, a more protracted team-building intervention. One of the practical ways in which these observations can be built on in either further process consultancy sessions or at a future team building activity is the production of ground rules to govern their behaviour. For example, I have used a version of Figure 2.2 to forbid their use by a team in their task of developing a strategy.

The next step

Having gathered the information via questionnaires, interviews and observations, the trainer has to draw some conclusions about the appropriateness of team building as an intervention. Generally, this decision-making process should be undertaken with the client. Therefore, the next stage should be a second meeting with the client.

Diagnosis

The objective of diagnosis is to identify the real problem(s) as opposed to the 'felt' need. What will be offered by all team members is not only a view about the problems, but also an explanation for their causes. Therefore, what will emerge from the analysis will be a cast of characters who are often conveniently labelled 'hero' or 'villain'. Similarly, problems will be ascribed to 'personality clashes', often described in terms that would suggest that these phenomena are independent of the individuals, i.e., some chemical process that poisons the air between person X and person Y. They are also described in fatalistic terms, i.e., inevitable and unchangeable. Such terms will also be applied to individuals who are accepted by the rest as 'characters'. In my experience, such 'characters' are not blessed with supportive or cooperative attributes. All of them display antisocial behaviours that are stoically accepted or excused by their colleagues. For most teams, there is an unerring consensus about the 'felt' problems and their causes. The expectation is that the trainer will see the team in the same way and produce the desired changes, preferably under anaesthetic!

Most trainers work with this simple 'causal' model of problems, e.g., the behaviour of X causes problems for Y and Z, therefore, if we change the behaviour of X, the problem will be resolved. Both in theory and practice, this position is untenable. The problem behaviour of X is a product of the relationship with Y and Z, therefore, the focus should include this wider picture. This would mean looking at the behaviours of both Y and Z that contributes to and helps sustain the behaviour of X. For example, my capacity to dominate members of a team in general discussion is going to depend on behaviours that will *allow* me to dominate, e.g., people staying quiet, not challenging my behaviour, etc. Unless this wider view is taken, the trainer will end up being seduced into helping to punish the 'villains' and 'supporting' the heroes, all of which behaviour is likely to lead to both sides becoming entrenched in their respective positions. A different perspective on these problems can be provided by systems theory.

Systems Theory

The basic assumption in Systems Theory[2] is that the nature and functioning of any organism (a human cell, a person, a team, an organization) can only be truly understood in the context of its relationship with the environment in which it exists. What unites this vast array of organisms is the fundamental drive for survival. In order to achieve survival, the organism will adapt, change, mutate, to changes in the environment on which it depends. For example, the human cell will respond to a virus (which is a change in its environment) by producing antibodies to protect itself. In making this response, the organism will attempt to achieve a form of balance, i.e., homoeostasis, that requires the least adaptation possible. If the threat is severe, however, the organism will take extreme action, which in itself might be counterproductive for its survival.

The team, as an organism, is not a single entity, but a complicated system that seeks the same kind of balance. At this level, the organism is not only concerned with the management of its external boundary with the environment. Additionally, it focuses on the management of its internal boundaries. The nature of these internal boundaries vary, but some of the fairly common ones are:

- age
- experience and knowledge
- openness
- competition
- expression of needs and feelings
- skills
- closeness
- safety
- support, etc., etc.

By their very nature, boundaries have the function of both including some people and excluding others. For example, the boundary of gender will create two groups, men and women. In terms of their day-to-day interactions and behaviours, individuals will be involved in managing these boundaries. At different times, certain boundaries will be enlarged by an individual and some or all of their colleagues will join them. For example, a team member offers a creative idea and a colleague will happily and explicitly build on the suggestion. At other times, an individual might attempt to push out a particular boundary and the attempt is resisted by a colleague. For example, the response to the creative idea is to poison it with scorn. By their nature, some of the boundaries are unchangeable, e.g., gender and age, but many boundaries that are *capable* of change become fixed and solid. A very common one in teams is the boundary of risk taking. All decisions and solutions that are reached by them are incremental rather than radical and this approach to problem solving and decision making can only be questioned at great cost to a new member.

The reality is that *all* these boundaries are being managed by *all* the members of the team, though it is often a common perception that a particular boundary is under the management of one or two people. It is not uncommon for a team to assign a particular boundary responsibility to an individual member, e.g., 'Old George is good at shooting down these new-fangled ideas. He's seen it all before.' What they lose sight of is that their behaviour actually *encourages* Old George in this role and is, therefore, equally important in managing this particular boundary. Hence, the emergence of 'characters' in teams.

Many 'personality clashes' in teams often start from, and centre on, a dispute over a particular boundary. If the trainer or team attempt to deal with the 'personality clash', the underlying boundary is liable to get lost, as is the potential resolution of the problem. To illustrate this point, a few years ago, I was working with a team of management trainers. During the process of analysis, there was a consensus that one of the major problems was a 'personality clash' between the two most senior and experienced members of the team—they were described as being in competition and intolerant of the contribution made by the other. The protagonists largely shared the same perception, each saying that the other was unwilling to move ground in the conflict. The non-combatants, as it were, studiously avoided taking sides, though they lamented the continuance of the problem and its effect on morale. At the event, they raised the problem, offered feedback to both individuals, then sat on the sidelines, waiting for one or the other to change. The protagonists gave each other feedback, with the result that neither moved from their original position. Stalemate and frustration reigned.

My own view is that this conflict concerned two key boundaries in the team that were significantly interrelated. The first boundary, was that of competition. There was open competition for both resources and the more interesting responsibilities and tasks. The second and, to me, more important boundary was implicit in their judgemental attitudes to each other. Their self-confidence was based on their sense of superiority, e.g., 'I am better than you, therefore I'm OK'. It was as if these two were acting out a dramatic dilemma for all the team. When I raised this perspective with the team, the other members of the team realized that, by answering their own dilemmas in these areas, the importance of the 'personality clash' was radically diminished. The other members of the team realized that their lack of self-confidence would not be resolved by comparing and competing with their senior colleagues, but by being willing to accept and respect their individual differences.

The consequence of the other members making these behavioural and attitudinal changes was that they changed the system in which the two senior members now had to operate. Although the two members never achieved a good relationship, the other members of the team, in general, were able to move forward and take their share of the responsibility for managing this particular boundary. My guess is that, had we stayed at the level of a 'personality clash', there would have been no resolution, but there would have been an *increased* level of intolerance and frustration.

A simple guideline for any trainer is that every problem in the team is shaped by a contribution made by each member. A system is not shaped by one person, not even the leader, but by the behaviours and attitudes of all. Therefore, to change a system involves as many people as possible being willing to take responsibility for making individual changes. In my experience, it is not necessary, though obviously it is desirable, for all members to change. When a significant number change, the system itself changes, which then makes it much more difficult for old behaviours and attitudes to flourish. This view provides an important counterbalance to the argument that a team will *only* change if *all* members are committed to such action (for some of the implications of this, see under Resistance below).

In returning to the client, it is advisable to offer a detailed summary of the 'felt' problems without breaching confidentiality of the interviews. As the client responds with either surprises or confirmations, I also offer my own observations about the significant boundaries that need addressing. I also invite the client to contribute to the diagnosis, not least to see if we share perceptions. The actual recommendation for moving ahead to the next stage should be a joint decision. Some important criteria for reaching this decision are listed in Figure 2.3.

---

1 That the team leader is both committed to the activity and is demonstrably willing to learn and change.

2 That there is a significant number of the team willing to genuinely undertake the activity. (A significant number should be more than half the team.)

3 That the trainer and the client share a similar diagnosis.

4 That the team has a common purpose, e.g., the management of a section, division or function or the delivery of a project.

5 That there is a certain level of support available for team members.

6 That there is no evidence or suggestion that an individual will seek to score points at the expense of colleagues.

Figure 2.3 *Criteria for team building*

Resistance Within these broad guidelines it is almost certain that the trainer will encounter some level of resistance from members of the team. The volume and degree of this will vary as it does on other training programmes. However, because of the nature of the event, certain interventions for dealing with resistance will not be appropriate. Some of these training choices, e.g., ignoring the person, inviting the views of others, having a discrete word outside the training room, subtle punishment and rewards, etc., are likely to inflame the situation on a team building event. The team are likely to oppose these interventions by the trainer.

Whatever form the resistance takes, the trainer needs to recognize that the team will have to work with this individual in future. They are likely, for this reason, to be very understanding and tolerant of their resistant behaviour. However, this forbearance is liable to switch to frustration if the resistant person is indulged. Listening to a person decrying the 'reality' of what is happening for a morning stretches the tolerance of even the most supportive colleagues, at which juncture, they are likely to punish the person and the trainer, then have a split in the group to deal with as well as the resistant individual.

Despite the resistance, it would appear to be axiomatic that any team building event should include all the team members. However, this is an axiom that my experience now refutes. In practice, to include someone who does not want to be included, for whatever reason, is counterproductive. What happens is that the individual demands a tremendous amount of attention for little return. The more efforts are made to include them, the more the person resists. The recommendation I make to all team leaders in the first interview is that, if a member of the team has reservations about attending the event, then they should be given permission not to go. However, at interview, the individual will also be told that their non-attendance will not, of itself, stop the event happening. Such a decision would only be reached if it was considered, after analysis, that an event would be inappropriate. The trainer should also talk through with the individual some likely consequences of their non-attendance. This will almost certainly involve them also experiencing some level of discomfort, isolation and a lack of involvement in the decisions that the team will take about their future functioning at the event.

Some of the individuals who fall into this category often entertain the hope that their opposition will be enough to ensure that the event will not take place. Once they realize that this bargaining position has gone, they are likely to shift position and be prepared to attend with 'an open mind'. The trainer would be well advised in such circumstances to demand a minimum contribution from the person at the event, e.g., they will not be allowed to reopen the discussion about the wisdom of having the event.

My experience of people who exercise their right not to attend is that the decision is no great surprise to the other members. In many cases, the decision reflects their general contribution, i.e., they are already semidetached and /or other members of the team see them as blockages. This choice actually brings to the fore an existing problem; it does not create a new one. Unfortunately, having raised the problem, it is hard for all parties to sweep it under the carpet. At the event itself, invariably the team make decisions to offer an invitation to the resister to become a fully contributing member. They are also likely to work out a back-up strategy should the invitation be declined.

There is always great consternation when this occurs. All the team members view the prospect of an event without the recalcitrant member as being severely flawed and, therefore, are likely to put great pressure on the trainer to make attendance compulsory. The chances of a conversion at the event are low and the idea is discarded only after the team has reached the limits of their energy and patience. The boundary issue that is being implicitly dealt with here is that of rejection. The member has decided to reject the team. Their decision not to attend merely makes this public. The rest of the team are unwilling to be rejected and/or to publicly reject. The first desire of most of the team is for the trainer to collude with them in seeking to avoid the issue. For example, 'Allow them to come and they will see that the event is productive'. If the trainer chooses to collude in this, then they are likely to be rejected and blamed by all parties during or after the event. If you take up this challenge as a trainer, make sure you succeed in arranging a conversion or be prepared to spend a lot of time dealing with the bad feelings that flow from failure. It is a challenge I find easy to resist! The possibility of this problem arising and the awkward choices that then have to be considered, is something I make clear at the first interview with the client. The leader already knows whether this problem is likely to arise in their team.

In addition, I will also tell the client at the same time that I might be returning after analysis with a recommendation that the event might be inappropriate for certain individuals. The kind of people I am concerned about fall into one of two types. The first type is the individual who would find it difficult to cope with what is being planned. The reason may be that they are particularly vulnerable to the slightest additional increase in the level of stress or uncertainty, because of personality or immediate circumstance. What I find in practice is that, by talking through the situation with them and agreeing explicitly on the kind of support that they might need from me or others, the individual invariably attends. The second type, however, rarely does. This is the kind of person who, for whatever reason, is abusive and destructive to their colleagues. While they are around, no one feels safe. When I make this judgement, I take responsibility for explaining my reasons to the person concerned.[3]

Assuming that there is a joint agreement between the client and the trainer to undertake a team building programme in general, they now have to agree on the most appropriate method to meet the need.

Implementation

In terms of implementation, the team building programme is the main focus. However, at this stage, it is worth both client and trainer already considering, as an integral part of the consultancy activity, a need to agree a review process. Hopefully, a number of review processes should naturally emerge from the event and should be the responsibility of the team. Additionally, the trainer should already be considering what review activity they would like to be involved in. There should be two purposes for the review:

1 in the light of experience, what additional service the trainer can offer the team
2 for both trainer and team to gain some hard information about the behavioural and attitudinal changes that have been achieved.

In considering these needs at this stage, the trainer should be able to agree with the team appropriate structures to provide this information (for suggestions, see appropriate sections in Chapters 4 to 6).

My experience is that the period of four to six months after the event provides ample time for the teams to have implemented their change strategies and have formed their judgements.

Summary

In this chapter, I have described process consultancy as a particular approach for gaining more information about a team and as a low-level form of team building intervention. I have also attempted to draw a clear distinction between the 'felt problems' identified by analysis and an approach to diagnosing the real problems drawn from Systems Theory. Finally, I have talked about problems that might be posed by team members and some of the difficult choices facing both the client and trainer. In the next chapter, I want to talk about some of the current approaches available for team building and offer a framework that enables a trainer to choose the right kind of approach for a team.

References

1 Schein, Edgar, *Process Consultation*, (2nd ed.) 2 vols. Addison-Wesley, 1988.
2 Phillips, Keri and Fraser, Tony, *The Management of Interpersonal Skills Training.* Gower, 1982.
3 Clark, Neil, *Managing Personal Learning and Change*. McGraw-Hill, 1990. See pp. 32–37 for a more detailed theoretical discussion of resistance and the choices available for handling it.

3 Approaches to team building

Introduction

As I mentioned in the Introduction, there is already a wealth of books and manuals available on team building. What is bewildering, however, is the best way for the trainer to relate these approaches to the needs of a particular team. It is possible to classify existing approaches as emanating from one of the following orientations.

- Approaches based on a particular model of team effectiveness. As one would expect, this type accounts for a great majority of the available literature. In this category I would include the approaches of John Adair,[1] The 'T-group' and the work of Wilfred Bion,[2] the Tavistock Approach,[3] etc.
- Approaches based on a particular methodology, e.g., outward bound approaches.
- Approaches that are a mix of the above, e.g., the work of Dr R.M. Belbin, which is both based on a view of an effective team and involves the use of a particular methodology, i.e., questionnaires. Margerison and McCann[4] have a similar approach.
- Because the above approaches involve using particular providers or paying for copyright material, there is a fourth approach that probably accounts for the vast majority of in-house team building. For want of a recognized name I shall refer to this as the 'Allsorts Approach'. What this actually includes is the product of trainers taking, or, to use the professional term, adapting some or bits of the above. What often underpins a particular programme is a scatter-gun approach, i.e., 'If Belbin doesn't make things happen, let's try Adair'.

One of the difficulties with all the above is the implicit, and often explicit, assumption that all these are appropriate for different kinds of teams in different stages of development. Often the only real criterion for choosing one of the above over the other is the personal preference or interest of the trainer. By their very nature, however, all existing approaches are limited by either their model of team effectiveness and/ or their choice of methodology. What is missing is some overview that could indicate the relevance of an approach to both a particular team and trainer. Those of us who have actually experienced and tried these approaches quickly learn that, whatever their intrinsic merits, they do not deal with certain kinds of problems. To illustrate some of these concerns, I would like to examine four popular approaches to team building. My intention in doing so is not to attempt to discredit the approaches, but to look at the implications for the trainer trying to use them with different kinds of teams.

Popular approaches to team building

John Adair At the heart of Adair's[1] approach to team building is a view of team effectiveness, which, at first sight looks remarkably like the approach of Edgar Schein (I will be describing the Schein approach later in this chapter). The approach can be shown as in Figure 3.1.

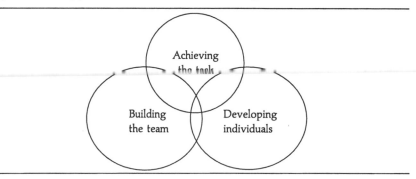

Figure 3.1 *Model of John Adair's approach*

The basis of the theory is that each group, like each individual, is unique. Therefore, what is relevant for one group may not work for another. However, all groups share three common needs:

1 to achieve the *task*—the task is what the group do or talk about, and is usually seen in terms of things rather than people
2 to build a *team*—Adair refers to this as a maintenance need of the group and it is primarily concerned with the relationships between people
3 meeting the needs of *individuals*—these needs (for physical satisfaction, security, self-esteem, self-actualization), if not satisfied, will impair the effective working of the group, but Adair registers an important caveat about the satisfaction of these needs:

> If such needs can be met *along with* and not *at the expense of* the group task and maintenance needs, then the group will tend to be more effective.[5]

This would appear to be an embracing view and one familiar to many trainers (in 1986, Adair claimed that one million managers had been through his programmes), but, very clearly, the extent to which trainers can work with this model is intended to be limited.

Generally, consultants in this field have approached teambuilding from a background of T-group or sensitivity training. They have imported all the assumptions of the Group Dynamics movement into their work, including . . . faulty assumptions about leadership.[6]

This caution is registered despite the fact that Adair earlier describes some of this theory as background information for managers to be aware of, although they must also avoid the dangers of playing the amateur psychologist. This would appear to be a very fine line to walk, i.e., be aware of, but do not use! The result of this caution is that what appears to be an overall framework for considering the effectiveness of the team is heavily biased towards developing skills primarily at the task and group level. This limitation is reinforced by his recommendation that team building exercises should employ 'substitute task variety', e.g., building towers with Lego bricks against profit margins. The value of the 'substitute task' is that the skills can be seen very clearly. However, the nature of such tasks for experienced management teams does not help to gain acceptance for team building. Also, it is difficult in practical terms to see how, in the context of building towers, it is envisaged that the manager may feel the temptation to be an amateur psychologist.

The trainer who uses this approach with teams that have dissatisfactions at both the group and individual levels are likely to find that the Adair approach causes some frustration for both team and trainer. For example, if two people in a team have a terrible relationship, the conflict will surface during an activity and there is no scope to deal with the problem except at the most superficial level. Any attempts to flit between the two levels of task skills and relationship problems, as the need arise, would actually be very difficult to achieve. In terms of both the task bias and the recommended use of substitute tasks, the Adair approach offers little headway in the effective management of any kind of process. The main learning method is the repetition of task skills.

The strength of Adair, however, is the clarity of a simple model— excluding the background group process theory—and its use for identifying and practising team skills. It is important, though, that trainers are aware that sometimes the simplicity of a model is not necessarily an advantage if you are trying to unravel a complicated problem. The involved interrelationships between these three goals is not adequately dealt with by Adair.

Outdoor training

Equally popular, though more controversial are the several varieties of outdoor training. There is a large and increasing number of suppliers who, whatever their differences, are united by the use of the outdoors as the method for learning. In a recent review of outdoor approaches, Mike Peckham[7] provides a very useful classification of their differences. He identifies four types:

1 *'The mountain top experience'* an approach that combines use of the outdoors with reviews, which are generally introspective and process-orientated; the emphasis is very much on personal development;
2 *'Now get out of that'* use of task solving problems and the outdoors with little attempt to relate to the work situation;
3 *'Games and simulations'* this combines task problem solving, in-depth reviews and theory reviews; the problem here is that the tasks may not appear real;

4 *'Equilibrium'* the characteristics of this approach are the provision of 'meaningful learning opportunities' combined with theory input and reviews.

My experience of the outdoors is that, like Adair, the strength of the approach is primarily at the skill and conceptual level if they accord to type 4, Equilibrium. However, the chances of achieving such a balance are very difficult. Trainers with experience in review skills are unlikely to have the skills and aptitude to cope with the outdoors. The secondary problem is that, despite their best efforts, the team is likely to be seduced by the task and will find it difficult to translate what it has learned so it can be used in the workplace.

The great advantage of the outdoor approach is the development of team spirit that occurs as a result of the achievement of the tasks. The development of skills at the group level is the greatest potential, for me, of this approach.

Meredith Belbin   Both the models of team effectiveness and the methodology associated with the approach were developed at Henley Management College. The research was initially carried out by observing the participants of management games. A comparison was made between those teams that were unsuccessful in completing the game and what Belbin describes as *Winning Teams*.[8]

On the basis of this comparison, the characteristics of Winning Teams are as follows:

- the person in the Chair fitted the description of the *Chairman* profile (see below), the characteristics of this role being someone who is patient but commanding, who generates trust, who looks for and knows how to use ability, does not dominate proceedings, knows when to pull things together and always works with the talented members of the group
- the team also contains a *Plant*, i.e., someone very creative and clever
- a particular spread of mental abilities, i.e., a clever Plant, another clever member, a Chairman who has slightly higher than average ability, while other members have slightly lower than average ability
- a good spread in team roles (see below)
- a good match between the attributes of members and their responsibilities in the team
- in the absence of certain team roles, the members adjust their contribution accordingly.

The team roles are listed in Figure 3.2.

- *Company Worker* Conservative, predictable and dutiful. Has organizing ability, common sense, discipline and is hard-working.
- *Chairman* Calm, confident, controlled. A capacity for treating all contributors on their merits.

- *Shaper* Highly strung, outgoing, dynamic. Has drive and a readiness to challenge inertia, complacency, self-deception.
- *Plant* Individualistic, serious-minded, unorthodox. Has genius, imagination, intellect, knowledge.
- *Resource Investigator* Extroverted, enthusiastic, curious and communicative. Has capacity to explore the new and respond to challenge.
- *Monitor/Evaluator* Sober, unemotional, prudent. Has judgement, discretion and hard-headedness.
- *Team Worker* Socially orientated, rather mild, sensitive. Has ability to respond to people and situations, and to promote team spirit.
- *Completer/Finisher* Painstaking, orderly, conscientious, anxious. Has capacity to follow through and is a perfectionist.

Figure 3.2   Team roles

Not surprisingly, Belbin places a lot of emphasis on the *selection* of teams and does not say a great deal about their *development*. Where the approach has been used in team building, the use of psychometric tests is an integral part of the programme. This raises a lot of practical and theoretical problems. At the theoretical end, the model must make sense to both trainer and team and this will spark the old 'nature v. nurture' debate. If I discover I am a Completer/Finisher, does this tell me who I am or merely what skills I have? At the practical level, what happens if the profiles for a team are heavily biased towards one category? Is the manager asked to reconsider the appointment of team members? Most organizations I work with do not have the flexibility to move people between teams.

In critiquing the approaches of both Belbin and Margerison and McCann, Robin Evenden and Gordon Anderson[9] make the cogent reservation:

However . . . we have all a repertoire, as well as preferences. If you have good all rounders in your team, who are able to perform different roles *when they are required*, then it will be successful. (My italics.)

Although there are some differences in approach between Belbin and Margerison and McGann, they all focus on the concept of identifiable team roles. (See Bibliography, p. 115.)

All these questions and discussion points, in my experience, are an unnecessary distraction to the team building activity. It is as if a hurdle is placed between the team and the event and, at some stage, all parties need to make the leap. However, my experience is that if it is used in a light way, i.e., as an introduction to the idea of roles within the team, it can provide a valuable intervention. Like both Adair and outdoors training, Belbin is used in conjunction with exercises that use substitute tasks, i.e., not the real tasks of the team. Interestingly, Belbin's suggestions on team building are limited to the manager changing the membership to increase effectiveness.

The Allsorts Approach

Most trainers, and many consultants, do not limit themselves to a particular approach, but develop one that they feel comfortable with. The actual programmes are usually an amalgam of underlying theory, not all of it internally consistent, and a mixture of methodology. Some of these programmes bear an uncanny resemblance to 'normal' programmes, which should more realistically be called something like 'Effective Team Working' or an 'Introduction to Management'—the kind of programme that could have the merit of being entertaining, but has little actual relevance to the needs of the team.

These trainers who have experimented with some or all of the above will be in danger of discarding these approaches because of their particular limitations, e.g., having to avoid or attempt to suppress a personality clash when using Adair, having pointless or surreal discussions about the problems that might arise for the team if their actual leader does not have the characteristics of the Chairman described by Belbin.

To avoid these limitations I will offer a view of teams that, first, enables a trainer to select an approach to team building that actually matches the needs of the team and, second, enables the trainer to draw on a range of theory and methodology within that approach (this includes Adair, outdoors training and Belbin). This view is based on the work of Edgar Schein.[10]

Edgar Schein

At first sight, the view of team effectiveness developed by Schein is deceptively similar to the Adair model, but the origin, and application, of the former provides far more flexibility and understanding for the trainer. One of the first significant pieces of research undertaken by Schein as a social psychologist, published in 1956, was entitled 'The Chinese Indoctrination Program for Prisoners of War: A Study of Attempted "Brainwashing" '.[11] This analysis of the use and abuse of group processes, albeit of groups *in extremis*, informs his research of groups within an organizational setting. Unlike John Adair, Schein's view is that the trainer or consultant working with any group needs not only to understand group processes, but also has to be able to intervene at that level to make a contribution to its maintenance or development. If there is a conflict, says Schein, then it is important to remember that the major determinant of effectiveness is the process. By contrast, the clear implication of Adair is that the trainer best ignore the process and stay at the level of skills.

I have no intention of reproducing here the theoretical base developed by Schein from his research, but I will attempt to offer a working summary of some of his key concepts.

The effective team

Like Adair, the basic model in Schein is that an effective team is one that recognizes and addresses three fundamental needs.

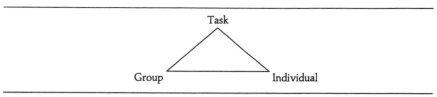

Figure 3.3 *The effective team*

As Figure 3.3 shows, these needs are to do with achieving the task, building or maintaining a cohesive group or expressing and satisfying individual needs or interests. Therefore, any and every piece of behaviour that takes place in a group can be said to be primarily directed at satisfying one of these needs.

Task behaviours The behaviours associated with attempting to achieve the task are:

- *initiating* the stating of goals or problems or proposals on how to proceed, which is often a leadership function, but, as groups develop, initiating behaviour may come from any group member
- *opinion/information seeking and giving* having suggested a goal and ways of proceeding, a logical next step is to exchange information and opinions. The quality of information exchanged and the time allowed for this activity are critical to the eventual solutions achieved and the commitment of the group
- *clarification/elaboration* these activities are important for a number of reasons: they check the adequacy of communication within the group; allow for the opportunity to combine and build on ideas to arrive at more creative and complicated solutions
- *summarizing* periodic summaries are important to ensure that ideas are not lost and to indicate whether or not there is a need to clarify and elaborate on any point
- *seeking or taking decisions* groups need someone to check periodically whether it is nearing a decision or still needs to discuss, e.g., 'Are we ready to decide?', and the success of this function depends on the sensitivity of the questioners.

Group behaviours In order for the group to survive and grow, it is necessary for the members to concern themselves with the maintenance of good relationships to ensure that all the resources within the group are contributing towards achieving the task. These group behaviours are:

- *gatekeeping* ensuring that members who have a contribution to make have an opportunity to make it even when more forceful or vociferous group members are present
- *encouraging* serves a similar function in terms of helping a person make their point, but also serves to create a climate of acceptance within the group
- *harmonizing and compromising* modifying personal views in the interests of the group or reducing tension by means of the use of humour.

(These are deliberately placed on the group rather than task side because they are useful in reducing destructive types of disagreements between members, but of limited use in achieving creative task solutions)

- *diagnosing, standard setting and testing* are most relevant as remedial measures when relationships have broken down to some extent. What the group then needs is some period of suspending the task while it diagnoses and seeks to resolve the process problems. It can also be used proactively to agree ground rules for communication and behaviour at meetings, e.g., 'The speaker is to finish before a reply can be made'.

Individual behaviours

Individuals bring to their membership of teams a range of needs and interests. If a team has not developed properly and is largely concerned with dealing with the task, then individuals are unlikely to take the risk of openly expressing their needs, interests and feelings. Instead, they will engage in self-orientated individual behaviours:

- *dominating others, being aggressive or blocking* individuals who are trying to assert their influence over the group or to resist the direction the group seems to be taking may express their self-interest in these ways. These responses may occur at any stage in the lifetime of a group when an individual feels that she or he is in some kind of competition
- *seeking help or recognition* individuals may seek support and establish a role for themselves in order to satisfy their anxieties, maybe making comments like, 'Go ahead and sort it out, it's all the same to me'. When they use this behaviour, they are also likely to portray themselves as purely rational, whereas the major problem with their colleagues are their irrational emotions, so they may describe themselves as willing to be team members if the others will play the game properly.

Findings

Typically, in my experience, the overwhelming majority of teams in organizations concern themselves not with the *three* needs, but only with one—the task. At a superficial level, this seems to be the only feasible method for working, particularly, where resources (including time) are very tight. Meetings of the team—which are generally to be seen as interruptions in the work of the individuals—should be fast, to the point and productive in terms of quantity and quality of outputs, be these outputs decisions, problems solved or information exchanged.

Process symptoms

Despite this task orientation, what actually happens is that, at meetings, frustration develops and becomes pandemic. Simple issues become robed in complexity and decisions are either avoided or forced through to no one's satisfaction. The process of the team, which can be clearly observed at meetings, is characterized by the following symptoms:

- grumbling outside meetings
- overt or implicit blaming of individuals or subgroups
- interpersonal competition (often lightly disguised in banter that has an edge to it)

- locked drawers, undisclosed information
- meetings that people dread and find any reason to avoid
- same old items on the agenda
- contributions polarized between high and low contributors
- tasks discussed but never completed
- jobs done many times
- lack of clarity about roles
- lack of creativity
- members do not ask for or offer help
- competition for resources is seen as normal
- individuals become isolated and do not develop.

As these and other symptoms become manifest, most teams then expect the leader to resolve the symptoms by becoming more 'decisive', i.e., autocratic. If the leader falls for this 'invitation', not having already succumbed because of their own impatience, they will become even more task-orientated, which will simply exacerbate the problems.

Individual needs in groups

One of the major contributors to this cycle is the unsatisfied needs that Schein says individuals bring to their membership of groups (see Figure 3.4).

Problems	Resulting feelings	Coping responses
1 Identity 'Who am I to be?'	Frustration	**A: 'Tough' responses** Fighting, controlling, resisting authority.
2 Control and influence 'Will I be able to control and influence others?'	Tension	**B: 'Tender' responses** Supporting, helping, forming alliances, dependency.
3 Needs and goals 'Will the group goals include my own needs?'	Anxiety	**C: Withdrawal or denial responses** Passivity, indifference, overuse of logic and reason.
4 Acceptance and intimacy 'Will I be liked and accepted by the group? How close a group will we be?'	Insecurity	

Figure 3.4   Needs in groups

In Schein's view, where the basic needs of membership are *not* met, the resulting feelings of frustration, tension and anxiety are likely to generate one of the three coping responses. Whereas Adair's view (see p. 30) is that the needs of individuals should only be addressed if to do so is not at the expense of task and group needs, quite clearly central to the view of Schein is the idea that the frustration of these needs will critically handicap the functioning of the team, so they *have* to be addressed.

In the way that it is possible to make predictions at the individual level about the consequences of behaviour, similar patterns can be predicted at the group level. Each team, according to Schein, is subject to a process of development. Within this process not only is it possible to identify key stages, but it is also possible to identify the key factors that determine how a particular team is likely to move between them.

Stages of group development

When a team is first assembled, the primary concern of all members is for safety, structure and guidance. In terms of satisfying these needs, members will look to the leader. This first stage Schein describes as *dependency*. The extent to which an individual is both able and willing to meet these needs is variable, as is the period of time required by members to find the requisite level of safety and structure. In organizations with a history of directive or authoritarian management, there is usually a nice match between the leader and the members and what should be a stage of development becomes an intrinsic part of the culture. For most teams, however, this should be a necessary, if transitory, period.

What will quickly emerge in any team is the reality of difference—of needs, views, styles. The issue facing the team is how to manage the inevitable conflict. In broad terms, if differences are managed effectively, the team will be characterized by their levels of both acceptance and creativity. If, however, this conflict is *not* handled effectively, then the team will begin to fragment. This stage Schein refers to as *counter-depedency*. The behaviours can be quite dramatic, with open conflict between leaders and members or between subgroups. The behaviour can also be less immediately obvious, i.e., overt conflict is suppressed into long and tedious discussions, the team has a chronic inability to make decisions, discussions are characterized by the continual use of 'Yes . . . ('What a great idea'), but . . . ('It will never fly')' contributions. Similarly, at this stage there could be a lot of blaming and scapegoating. There might, paradoxically, even appear to be a consensual view as to the identity of the villain. There is also likely to be a knowledge of task skills, but an unwillingness to use them.

The team that works through this stage often develops rules or norms of behaviour, e.g., 'Only one person is allowed to speak at once', 'We must never interrupt anybody'. Although the purposes of the rules are healthy, i.e., a desire to include everyone, they are often used in an unproductive way. Members police, and are policed by, the rules. There is an expectation that, as a member of this team, one must behave in approved ways and eschew certain other behaviours, e.g., obstinately sticking to a point of view, the open expression of feelings. In the context of groups on residential programmes, this stage of *cohesion* is most evident when the group apparently has to do everything together, e.g., eat, drink, have fun, stay up or retire. Typically, individual members are reluctant to defy the perceived will of the group. Again, this should be a stage of development that is worked through.

The next, and final, stage is described by Schein as *interdependence*. The move to this stage is signalled by the awareness and acknowledgement of individuality. There is less desire to patrol the commonality of membership—individuals are free to come and go. Their actions and behaviours are not scrutinized for implied or overt statements of disloyalty, but are trusted to be contributing to the corporate good. This stage is also the period when individuals not only feel able to consciously develop their skills, but to do so by learning from the actions and behaviours of their colleagues. One feature of the preceding stages is a concern to make judgements in terms of rights and wrongs. This is now replaced by a desire to learn from the outcomes of individual and collective behaviour.

Unfortunately, the assumption on the part of most teams in most organizations is that the prevailing 'norm' of team life is that described by interdependence, but the reality is that the majority are stuck in the first two stages. Although the Schein model implies a continuing movement of development for any team, this is not axiomatic.

A similar process of development for individuals roughly equates to this model of *group* development. At a personal level, *childhood* is comparable to dependency, *adolescence* to counterdependency, *early adulthood* to cohesion and *maturity* to interdependence. At the personal level, it is possible to identify adults who remain stuck in the phase of dependency on all or any authority figures. They will only do what they are told to do and will not take the risk of using their initiative. It is also possible to identify people who are always looking to take on and fight any display of authority. Such people are sometimes referred to as rebels without a cause. People who get stuck at the comparable stage of cohesion are characterized by their overwhelming desire to identify with, and seek approval from, a particular peer group. Sociologically, such groupings are appearing all the time (whatever happened to the Yuppies?). The number of individuals who do get through to the final stage of maturity often appear to be the exception. The best definition of maturity that I have heard goes like this: it is that stage in life when the individual is able to accept themselves without judgement and is able to accept others on the same basis.

At the individual level, those who get stuck at a particular stage need some kind of dramatic event or intervention to move them on (for example, redundancy, divorce, change of career, a new partner). Without such an impetus, the normal ebb and flow of life will have little impact on that person, they have learned to cope with these influences.

Teams, once they are stuck, are unlikely to move forward (hence, the number of ineffective teams in organizations). The kinds of events likely to affect the movement of teams include:

- change of membership
- change of leader
- major change in working practices
- work pressures
- reorganization
- the appearance of an outside threat.

For example, a team that has spent unproductive months involved in counterdependency suddenly move into cohesion when the personnel department introduces a new job evaluation scheme. The team coalesce against the common enemy for the duration. When the enemy is defeated, however, the team will revert to its former state. In the same way, the spirit of the Blitz did not survive long after 1945.

Central to Schein's view of teams is the belief that the effectiveness of teams is determined not by the level of task skills available to leaders and members, but by their awareness of, and skills in, the process. Therefore, team building interventions by the trainer or the manager may need to address process issues at either the group or individual level.

My experiences in team building have made me aware of the fact that the problems that a particular team experience can be seen to emanate from three separate areas of team effectiveness:

- *task* skills
- *group* process
- *individual* process.

The approaches that I looked at earlier in the chapter either emphasize one particular area (e.g., Belbin and group process, outdoors training and task skills) or imply that they are applicable to all three areas (e.g., Adair).

Three generic approaches

However, what the trainer discovers when working with any training group is that choosing to intervene at these three levels requires different kinds of skills and will involve different levels of risk. For example, teaching a group how to solve problems creatively is different in kind to helping a group to become aware of its process. Equally, there is a palpable difference between the latter and helping individuals become aware of the consequences of their behaviour for colleagues. At each stage in this sequence, the risk level for both the learner and the trainer has increased substantially. What also changes at each level is the choice of learning vehicle (e.g., substitute task for problem solving as opposed to examining the actual behaviour of the group). There is also a change in the time frame for learning (e.g., there and then for group process as opposed to here and now for individual learning).

In the context of a normal management training programme, the incorporation of these different levels can be part of the design structure, i.e., establishing security at a low risk level preparatory to moving to personal learning in a here and now format. This model of learning for a stranger group is not applicable to a working team. There already exists within the team differential levels of risks in the relationships, e.g., A is more open to B than she is to C or D. Equally important, members will want to keep these differences without necessarily wishing to acknowledge them. In a stranger group this is not usually a problem.

In addition, every team I have worked with knows the level of risk that is required to move the team forward. If the trainer comes in at too low a level, the team members' anxiety and excitement about the event will quickly turn into frustration and indifference. If the intention is to raise the risk level later, both team and trainer will experience a dreadful feeling of suspense. The trainer who comes in at too high a level will encounter equal mixes of anger and fear. Whatever the difference in feelings, the end result will be the same—rejection of the trainer and the event.

The diagnosis should have identified the appropriate level for intervention and the necessary risk level required. If there is more than one level, then it is recommended that the trainer intervene at the higher level first (say the group), with a view to working later at the lower level (of the task). The basis of this recommendation, as every trainer discovers, is that if there are any kinds of process issues in a group, then any attempt at a skill-level intervention is pointless. The learning activity will be sabotaged by those with unfinished business. By anticipating the higher risk early—preferably at the analysis and diagnostic stage—there is greater time available for all to manage the risk at an earlier point in the consultancy activity, i.e., in discussions and preparatory work for team members.

Of course, the major problem with the Allsorts Approach is not the mix of theory, but the often dislocated sense of movement between the different methodologies and their respective risk levels. Going from skills exercises to identifying group process and back again, creates unnecessary blocks to learning. It is difficult to achieve any sense of completion if you are struggling with this kind of mental and emotional dislocation.

The trainer who operates on the basis of 'going with the flow' of the team is either blessed with an enviable omnipotence or an inconsiderate ignorance (I have met many trainers who fall into the latter category; I have yet to encounter an example of the former). Such lack of structure is a reflection of the trainer's lack of understanding and knowledge. By contrast, the trainer who is able to determine the appropriate level for intervention is demonstrating respect for the team and themselves as a professional.

Summary

In this chapter I have considered some of the existing approaches to team building. In discussing their distinguishing features, I have tried to indicate not only their strengths and weaknesses, but also some of the problems of working with teams generally. In describing some of the major contributions that Edgar Schein has offered to our understanding of both group effectiveness and processes, I have suggested that this provides us with a starting point to identify three generic approaches to team building, each characterized by distinct learning aims, risk levels and methodologies. These three approaches—task, group and individual—will be described in the following three chapters. For each approach I will describe:

- diagnostic factors for choosing this approach
- training methodologies
- design and structural features
- ground rules
- exercises and theory
- interventions by the trainer
- problems and how to handle them.

References

1 Adair, John, *Effective Teambuilding*. Gower, 1986.
2 Bion, W. *Experiences in Groups: And Other Papers*. Tavistock Publications, 1968.
3 De Board, Robert, *The Psychoanalysis of Organizations*. Tavistock Publications, 1978.
4 Margerison, Charles, and McCann, D., *Team Management*. Mercury, 1990.
5 Adair, John, op. cit., p. 62.
6 Adair, John, op. cit., p. 137.
7 Peckham, Mike, 'Management Development and the Outdoors', Part 1, in *Training and Development*, pp. 17–18, May 1993.
8 Belbin, Dr R.M., *Management Teams: Why They Succeed or Fail*. Heinemann, 1981.
9 Evenden, Robin, and Anderson, Gordon, *Making the Most of People*. Addison-Wesley, 1992.
10 Schein, Edgar, *Process Consultation* (2nd ed.) 2 vols. Addison-Wesley, 1988.
11 Schein, Edgar, 'The Chinese Indoctrination Program for Prisoners of War: A Study of Attempted "Brainwashing",' in *Psychiatry*, 1956, XIX, pp. 149–172.

4 The task approach

Diagnostic factors

The task approach is primarily concerned with the accomplishment of the goals and responsibilities of the team. The particular behaviours to be identified and explained include:

- initiating—the stating of goals, problems or proposals on how to proceed
- opinion/information seeking and giving
- clarification and elaboration
- summarizing
- seeking or taking decisions.

Therefore, the learning goals based on the development of these behaviours would include:

- clarity of information generation and exchange
- problem solving discipline and skills
- ability to make clear decisions
- an ability to plan and manage meetings
- skills of creativity.

In undertaking the analysis and diagnosis, there should be a consensus among all members that problems stem from a lack of skills. The leader and the group are well-intentioned but frustrated by a perceived lack of progress, which is often exacerbated by tight time constraints. Typically, the kinds of teams for which this is most appropriate include those shown in Figure 4.1.

- Newly formed teams. Particularly project teams which have a fixed-term period to complete a task. This kind of event will provide a kick-start into working effectively.
- Inexperienced teams. Those in which individuals and, particularly, the leader are relatively new to team working.
- Teams characterized by an inability to make decisions, a lack of structure for managing meetings effectively, a lack of good working practices, a lack of innovation and an inability to solve problems.
- Teams that have little, if any, unfinished business among their members or with the leader.

Because of the nature of the approach teams of 6 to 20 members can be accommodated.

Figure 4.1   The types of teams—task

The diagnosis will reveal that many teams are characterized by an absence of these skills, but it is the *reason* for their absence that is important. If there are problems at the process level (group or individual), then the first casualty is often the task skills of individual members. If the diagnosis reveals process problems at either level, it would be most unwise to proceed with a task approach. Although it is tempting, particularly for the trainer new to team building, to imagine that the provision of skills will provide some answers, in practice it is likely to merely add to the frustration. Participants on such events will be too aware of the unresolved issues and a strong cynicism of the learning approach is likely to develop. The trainer will also experience a strong sense of being on the edge of an abyss. Under such circumstances, the trainer would be advised to go in at either the group or individual level with a view to adding on the task skills later as part of the design.

Administration

Ideally, all team building events should be off-site and residential, but successful task-based programmes can be run on a non-residential basis. The kind of programme described in this chapter is designed for a group of 12 (the optimum size), with 1 or 2 trainers, and to be run over 3 days. If the team is nearer to the maximum size of 20, then 2 trainers would be the minimum and the length would increase to 4 days.

Methodology

The basic methodology of this approach is the identification and practising of task skills. At the earliest opportunity—at the first meeting with the client, if possible—the trainer should make it clear to all parties that the focus is the development of skills and that feedback will be limited to this context. Having explained the approach to the leader, the best way to reinforce the message is through the production and distribution of a programme on completion of the diagnosis. This will also substantiate and amplify any description offered to members at interview. (It is conceivable that the processes of analysis and diagnosis actually indicate that a completely different approach to team building is called for. When this happens, it is vital that the trainer then goes to see all team members before the event to tell them what has happened and explain the revised proposal.)

Preparatory work

Although, like most trainers, I am generally reluctant to ask groups to undertake preparatory work, in the case of team building there are good reasons to make an exception. The first is that it is imperative that members think through the possibilities before the event (not least to consider the issue of risk level instead of having to cope with the experience at the time). The second is that anticipation arouses specific expectations. The third, and this will also be reinforced by knowledge of a review process, is that it will bring home the message that team building is designed to lead to observable behavioural and attitudinal changes.

The kind of task that I set for teams is designed to encourage them to think and be analytical. For example:

Based on your experiences of being in teams as members and or leaders, please write down your answers to the following:

- effective teams do the following things . . .
- ineffective teams do the following things . . .

At the event you will be asked to read out your answers.

It does not matter if team members discuss these questions among themselves, though, as a trainer, I make it clear that I will want to hear from each person at the event as well. An alternative could be the use of the team effectiveness questionnaire (see Figure 1.2, p. 13).

The intention of this, or a similar task, would be to discourage the individual from exploring their feelings about being a member of the team. One of the concomitants of the task approach is for the trainer to patrol the boundary between thought and feelings all the way through the team building process, with a view to staying within the thinking area. For these reasons, I would be very reluctant to look at the areas of leadership and membership with this approach because it will be hard for individuals to effectively separate the 'content issue' of leadership from the 'process issue' of X as leader.

Design features

Of the three approaches, this is the nearest to the design of a conventional management skills programme. The learning approach should be based on the cycle shown in Figure 4.2.

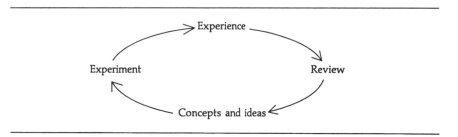

Figure 4.2 Learning cycle

The trainer can choose to intervene in this cycle from any of the four points (whether this be in the form of an exercise/activity, theory input, group discussion or whatever) and, during the programme, should certainly vary the starting point for each session. For example, start the problem solving session with a theory input, but start the creativity session with an exercise. My experience of working with trainers on all kinds of team building is that the element of this learning model that trainers try to avoid is that of providing theory inputs. Their own discomfort about doing so is rationalized away by the view that theory from the trainer intrudes on, and somehow impairs, the group's learning. The reality, in my experience, is that teams need maps they can use to understand the rest of the training experiences.

At a design level, the issue of responsibility for learning must be tackled. In broad terms, this should mean that the trainer clearly, and explicitly, relinquishes control from the start of the programme. For the programme to work, the trainer needs to fill the leadership gap (see the stage of dependency, Chapter 3) *and* allow space for the team to fill it, too. This gap *must* be filled by the *team*, not the leader. If the leader takes this role, then the event is merely helping to develop dependency in the team. The trainer can start offering this opportunity from the point of introduction of the ground rules (see below).

One of the dilemmas, touched on in the previous chapter, is the use of 'real' as opposed to 'substitute' tasks. In the *early* stages of this approach, then, the latter is a preferable choice because it shows the skills that you are focusing on without any distraction. However, the content at the *end* of the programme should be on the real tasks and procedures of the team. This not only helps to validate the earlier activity, but helps to provide the material for the action planning and subsequent review.

This view is part of a principle of design for these kinds of programmes, i.e., to start from the *general* (e.g., What is a team?) and work towards the *particular* (e.g., 'What will this team be doing differently back at work tomorrow?'). For the same reason, the sequence of the learning goals listed on p. 43 would provide a logical structure for the programme, i.e.:

information exchange ➡ problem solving ➡ decision making ➡ planning and running meetings ➡ creativity.

In describing exercises and theory to be used, I will be following this sequence. However, before then, it will be appropriate to look at the start of such a programme and, in particular, the ground rules.

The ground rules   The introductory activities (introductions and ground rules) are important not for exchanging information, but for beginning to deal with the uncertainty and speculation that has developed since the last contact with the team. It is typical of team building that the behaviour of the group at the first meeting on the event is liable to be marked by some hysteria and/or aggressiveness towards the trainers (although this is invariably evident on process-based programmes, it can also occur on task-based programmes). This mixture of feelings can often lead the group to encourage the trainer to 'get on with' the programme as the method for dealing with their anxiety. A better response is for the trainer to spend time on the introductory activities. The particular format for introductions for this level is to ask each person to make a statement, including:

• what I would like this programme to achieve is . . .

and

• the concerns that I have about the event are . . .

The trainer would log the replies on flipchart paper, then introduce the ground rules as the first step in the process of responding to both lists.

The purpose of the ground rules is to create a learning climate by attempting to clarify roles and responsibilities. The ground rules most appropriate for this kind of event are:

- everything that takes place on the event is confidential to the group, i.e., they will have a responsibility to communicate to others about their deliberations, but, as part of the activity, *they* will decide *what*, to *whom* and *when* these will be made
- the aims of the event are:

  —to develop their understanding of effective working in teams
  —to identify and practise the particular skills of team working

- the role of the trainer is to provide structure, guidance, feedback and theory
- the role of the group is to take part in activities and discussions and to give and receive feedback after activities
- the feedback activities will be structured by the trainer and will be limited to the behaviours used by participants on the events
- learning involves joint responsibility, with both sides carrying out their roles
- the learning approach will involve the group carrying out activities (some real tasks, some training tasks), reviewing their performances and giving feedback, sharing their ideas and reaching decisions and jointly planning the future operation of the team
- the aim of the programme is to provide them with ideas and experiences to enable them to choose the best approach for their team.

The concerns that the group have identified that are not addressed by these ground rules should now be used to add to this list. For example, if one of the expressed concerns is, 'That people will take the experience too personally', then I would invite the team to formulate a rule to avoid this possibility occurring. This, in effect, may be simply adding the following to the list:

- no one to take the experience too personally

or, more specifically:

- when feedback is offered, the giver is to check with the receiver whether or not they understand what has been said.

The more ground rules a team formulates in this way, the sooner they begin taking responsibility for themselves and their learning. Their additions enable them to take ownership of all the ground rules more easily.

Occasionally, I supplement the above list with rules to take account of particular circumstances. For instance, if there is some degree of anxiety about being asked to perform in activities, I will include a couple of the following specific permissions:

- it's OK to make mistakes
- I don't have to prove that I am either the best or worst member of this group.

After some experience of team building management trainers, I have learned that adding the following:

- I can speak in English
- I can suppress my need to write on flipcharts

can greatly improve communication in their groups!

The exercises and theory

Having completed the introductory activities, the first task would be to ask members of the team to read out their answers to the preparatory questions (if this has not been set, I would split the team into buzz groups to identify characteristics of effective and ineffective groups). The answers will not only provide the trainer with an idea of the conceptual level of the groups, but also the first opportunity to work together. At some stage in this activity, the group will apply their content answers to the way they are working together on this task.

Their report back provides the trainer with the opportunity to offer some theory of team effectiveness. The choice of model is less important than the fact it would be wise to stay at the skill level. For this reason, I would choose the Adair model in preference to others because of its task bias, and I would not elaborate beyond the description in Chapter 3. What is useful, at this stage, particularly for teams new to the skills, is to offer a behavioural framework that can be used to review team activities that will take place. A good simple model that is consistent with Adair is Behaviour Analysis, developed by Neil Rackham.[1]

This framework was originally developed by Rackham and his colleagues as an instrument for evaluating the outcomes of supervisory training. It was subsequently used by them as the basis for programmes in supervisory skills and what is listed in Figure 4.3 is the 11-category version.

- *Proposing* behaviour putting forward a new suggestion.
- *Building* behaviour that extends or builds on someone else's.
- *Supporting* conscious declaration of support.
- *Disagreeing* conscious and reasoned disagreement.
- *Defending/attacking* behaviour that attacks or defends.
- *Blocking/difficulty stating* for example, 'It won't work!'
- *Open* behaviour that exposes the individual to ridicule, e.g., 'I don't understand'.
- *Testing understanding* checking whether or not people have understood a contribution.
- *Summarizing* e.g., 'What we seem to be saying . . .'.
- *Seeking information* e.g., 'Tell me more about your idea'.
- *Giving information* e.g., 'I think we ought to . . '.

Figure 4.3 *Behaviour analysis*

These categories can be amended or added to in response to local circumstances. The framework is designed to stay at the level of observable behaviour and is not intended to be used as a vehicle for exploring group or individual process. It is also designed to be used quantitatively, i.e., each behaviour of a member is scored. So, at the end of a meeting, the feedback for individuals provides a numerical profile of their contribution. By adding the individual scores together, the group profile produced provides a useful diagnosis of problems, e.g., a very high score on proposing with correspondingly low scores on building, supporting and testing understanding will help to explain a team's inability to progress discussions. Appropriate action steps to remedy the problem are also self-evident, i.e., the conscious use of specific behaviours.

My experience of using this framework with all kinds of groups is that the categories are readily understood and, *provided that it is kept at the level of description rather than explanation* it meets the framework's professed need to be safe, i.e., people do not get upset offering or receiving this kind of feedback. Without a framework for discussing behaviour, the team will use its own language, which is likely to include not only descriptive but also interpretative and evaluative terms, e.g., 'She is being defensive', 'That comment was most unhelpful'. In addition to providing a common, relatively safe language, it also encourages individuals to develop greater awareness of their own patterns of contributions, e.g., *giving* rather than *asking for* information.

Having explained the framework and the relevance of the different behaviours to effective group working, future reviews can be structured with this kind of feedback. The best use involves two or more members dropping out of different activities and each taking responsibility for scoring the behaviours of half the team. Because the observer roles are rotated, everyone has a chance to develop their understanding of the categories. For a similar reason, it would be appropriate to record on closed circuit television (CCTV) at least one of the tasks (both the problem solving and decision making activities described later would be appropriate). However, it is only with task approaches to team building that I would choose to use this valuable learning medium—and, even here, only sparingly. The reasons for this caution are, first, that it increases the risk levels for participants, second, that, in combination with substitute tasks, it adds another unwanted layer of artificiality and, third, the technology can intrude on the learning by slowing down the pace and/or altering the atmosphere of the group. For example, team members will choose to agree with each other that the recorded behaviour is 'untypical', i.e., irrelevant.

Information exchange

The purpose of this exercise is to practise the skills of information collection and exchange in the course of completing a task to a deadline. The observers will be asked to pay particular attention to how information is managed by the group members and the extent to which individuals are included or excluded during the course of the task. There are a number of exercises available to look at this area. The particular features of this design are:

- the outcome is a physical product that is not dependent on any particular skills or abilities, therefore, no one should be disadvantaged
- the time and resource constraints in the exercise will be familiar problems
- it involves the group physically moving away from their seated positions and provides them with an opportunity to crawl over the floor, i.e., unobtrusively invite the team to push out the boundaries of formality.

The task is called 'Design Project' and the briefing is given below.

Design Project

Briefing

> This team has 45 minutes to design a scale diagram of the training room with movable representations of the furnishings. Your diagram must be of a sufficient standard to enable the trainer(s) to experiment with different layouts of the room.
>
> At the end of 45 minutes, you will be asked to present your diagram and explain the approach that you adopted to completing this task.

Notes

Typically, teams make assumptions (e.g., to use imperial rather than metric measures, or vice versa), do not agree on who is responsible for collecting what information, realize too late that once members have split up for their various tasks it is exceedingly difficult to communicate.

Although the focus of the exercise—in this context—is on communication, it begins to open up wider issues about structuring themselves to carry out tasks and their approach to problem solving.

Problem solving   The choice of exercises in this category is endless, but *The Encyclopedia of Team Building Activities* edited by J. William Pfeiffer,[2] and, Mike Woodcock's *50 Activities for Teambuilding*[3] are good sources. You could make it either a 'classroom' or outdoors activity. If there is enough time available, then the selection of two contrasting problems is worth while, e.g., a closed task, where there is one answer, and an open-ended problem, where a number of options are available. An example of the former is the 'Shoe Shop Problem' (this is an Anglicized version of an exercise in *The Encyclopedia of Team Building Activities* mentioned above).

Shoe Shop Problem

Briefing

> A man went into a shoe shop to buy a pair of shoes costing £12. He handed the shop assistant a £20 note. It was early in the day and the shop assistant did not have any change. He took the £20 note and went to the restaurant next door where he exchanged it for a mixture of notes and coins. Later that morning, the restaurant owner came to the shop assistant and said, 'This is a counterfeit £20 note'. The shop assistant apologized profusely and took back the counterfeit note and gave the restaurant owner two good £10 notes.
>
> Not counting the cost of the shoes, how much did the shoe shop lose?

Note   The answer is £8.

An example of an open-ended problem to use would be 'Construct a Game'.

Construct a Game

Briefing

> The team has 60 minutes to construct a game suitable for four to six adults to play. The criteria for the game are, first, that it can only be played outdoors and, second, that all artefacts required to play the game must be naturally available in the environment (i.e., no breakages or damage allowed).

Between these last two activities, it would be advisable to ask the team to generate a check-list for problem solving and/or for the trainer to provide a theory input. Again, the choice of model is less important than the fact that the team has one to work with. For example, the input shown in Figure 4.4 regarding a systematic approach is more than appropriate.

- *Understanding* clarifying the nature of the problem and organizing to work effectively.
- *Objectives* agreeing a clear statement of what needs to be achieved.
- *Success criteria* agreeing a measure to test whether or not the objective has been achieved.

- *Information* identifying and collecting the necessary information.
- *Planning* agreeing a step-by-step plan of action.
- *Action* carrying out the plan.
- *Review* reviewing the action taken to learn from the experience.

Figure 4.4   *A systematic approach to problem solving*

The advantages of providing the theory in between the exercises is that the team have a chance to try out this approach. Looking at problem solving by means of these kinds of exercises will inexorably give rise to discussions about the process of decision making.

Decision making   It is useful to identify the ways in which teams make decisions and, equally important, the ways in which teams *avoid* making decisions. This can either be done through a group discussion or a theory input (see p. 20–1, ff. and Figure 2.2 for material to use).

When I have worked with teams that have not only told me in the analysis that they were hopeless at making decisions *but* then demonstrated this lack of aptitude at the event, I have found the following exercise to be particularly useful.

Avoid Making a Decision

Briefing

> This team has 25 minutes to avoid making any decisions and to record as many ways as possible that this can be achieved.

Notes   The interesting outcome from this task—after some bewilderment—is that the team end up making a decision, even if it is a decision not to complete the task. The inherent paradox helps to dispel the self-fulfilling prophecy that teams with this problem tend to adopt. Part of the reason for this is a lack of understanding about the range of choices available. Teams approaching this area often focus on polarized choices, i.e. autocracy and democracy (always defined in majority voting terms).

Based on my experience with teams, the idea of consensus *as a genuine exploration of differences* appears to be an alien concept. For this reason I choose a 'Consensus Exercise' like the following to explore their understanding.

Consensus Exercise

Briefing

Please read each of the following statements carefully and:

- individually, either agree (A) or disagree (D) with the statement
- the team will then have 30 minutes to reach a consensus decision on the statements, again scoring A or D.

The statements are as follows:

1 In a group with a strong leader, an individual is able to achieve greater personal security. A or D

2 Leadership is the intelligent control of group activity rather than just getting others to follow you. A or D

3 When the leader is doing their best, one should not openly criticize and find fault with their conduct. A or D

4 Generally, there comes a time when democratic methods must be abandoned in order to solve practical problems. A or D

5 In the long run, it is more important to use democratic methods than to achieve specific results by other means. A or D

6 It is sometimes necessary to ignore the feelings of others in order to reach a decision. A or D

7 By the time the average person has reached maturity, it is almost impossible for that person to increase their skill in group participation. A or D

8 Silent members constitute a threat and a nuisance to the group. A or D

9 Conflict is not the expression of differences in individuals, but of their failure to make their differences contribute to the common good. A or D

10 A group functions most efficiently when it ignores rather than discusses rivalries between members. A or D

Notes The purpose of this exercise is not to 'sell' the virtues of consensus to a team, but to allow them to experience an attempt to work in this way. Such an exercise shows the respective merits of the different categories identified by Rackham. The difference of impact where teams experience a lot of disagreeing/blocking, compared to experiences of testing understanding.

At this stage in the programme, it is a good idea to move away from substitute tasks and start addressing some of the issues of team performance. The skill area for doing this is the planning and preparation of meetings. It also provides an opportunity to apply the skills already practised in other areas.

Planning and preparing for meetings

At no stage in the programme has any distinction been made between the team leader and other members of the team. In this sense, they have been treated like a normal training group. As a precursor to moving on to a real task, the trainer needs to have spent time with the leader, discussing the process of decision making that now takes place. I recommend to the leader, and then inform the team, that, in the following discussion, the aim is to achieve decisions, if not through consensus, then certainly through a majority vote. The only special position allocated to the leader is to state clearly, and unequivocally, whether or not a particular proposal is acceptable or not. This fail-safe position, in my experience, has only been exercised rarely, and then in response to information that other team members did not have.

With this background, the team are asked to undertake the 'Effectiveness of Meetings' task.

Effectiveness of Meetings

Briefing

> This team has 90 minutes in which to make proposals to improve the effectiveness of meetings. The team can organize itself in whatever way is appropriate, e.g., splitting into subgroups for part of the time, having a chairperson or not, etc. At the end of this period, however, the team should have agreed specific proposals by either consensus or majority vote.

Notes

Because of the nature of this task, it is suggested that observation be undertaken by the trainer and feedback be offered at the end of the meeting. To aid their deliberations, I sometimes offer the points shown in Figure 4.5 for consideration.

---

1 *Preparation* What preparation is required by members and leaders? Production of agendas, minutes, supporting papers?
2 *Membership* Who needs to attend? Will they have special roles and responsibilities?
3 *Agenda* What items need to be addressed? Are items for information, discussion, decision making? Should a time be set for the meeting? Should agenda items be timed?
4 *Venue* Where should the meeting be held? What seating arrangements are appropriate?

5 *Roles* What are the differences in roles between leader and member? What is the decision-making process?

6 *Actions* Will minutes be kept? How will action points be recorded? What are the responsibilities of members to inform other people or teams?

7 *Review* What procedure is required to review the effectiveness of the meeting? What can be applied at future meetings?

Figure 4.5 *Planning meetings*

Notes The decisions that the team reach obviously form one of the key elements of both the action planning and the team building review process. If the team become stuck at this stage then the logical way forward is to revisit the skill areas already covered on the programme. If the problem is an emerging process issue, some options for dealing with this are listed under the heading Problems and how to handle them later in this chapter.

Creativity If only in terms of including a variety of activities, it makes sense to move on to the area of creativity next. A good option for exploring this is to go straight into an exercise using a substitute activity. If the team are feeling good about their achievements, then one way in which this can be built is to offer a task to develop their identity, such as the following, 'Team Identity'.

Team Identity

Briefing

The task of this team is to make a statement about your identity. Some examples of the ways in which you can make this statement are:

- a short play (no more than five minutes long)
- a picture or series of pictures
- a song or poem
- a mime
- any combination of the above.

Notes If the trainer detects that the team has unfinished business regarding any element of the programme or in the group then they would be better advised to use a different task. A task such as the following one would be a good choice.

Logo

Briefing

> The team has 60 minutes to design a new logo for the organization, with the following conditions:
>
> • the design must be free-standing and made from the enclosed collection of Lego bricks
> • other materials available may be incorporated into the design
> • the design must be radically different from any previous or present logo.

The important element in this task is the *last* condition that, because it is asking people to think about what is, makes it hard for them to be creative. What tends to happen is that teams do produce something, but it is only marginally different.

In reviewing either of these last two exercises, a useful structure is to ask them to identify:

• which group behaviours aided creativity
• which group behaviours inhibited creativity?

Building on their learning points the trainer can now usefully offer some creativity techniques, such as those given in Figure 4.6.

The aim of the following techniques is to shake free from traditional logical approaches to dealing with problems. By deliberately breaking existing patterns creative solutions or ideas are likely to emerge.

Brainstorming

Procedure

1 Identify the problem, e.g., 'How to cross a stream'.
2 For an agreed period of time—ten minutes, for example—simply generate as many alternatives as possible *no matter how absurd*, e.g., swim across, build a bridge, fly, etc.
3 No one is allowed to *comment* on any suggestions made during this period.
4 At the evaluation stage—40 minutes after starting, for example—each listed alternative is treated as a starting point for a new solution, e.g., what *kind* of bridge—materials, structure, size, etc.

Analogies

Procedure

1 Identify the problem, e.g., 'How to learn a new job'.
2 Generate analogies, e.g. 'Teaching an old dog new tricks', 'Nothing ventured, nothing gained', etc.

3 Pick one analogy and brainstorm solutions. For example, 'Teaching an old dog new tricks' may include:

- use a cat
- use chocolate
- use the boot, etc.

4 Then relate each of these solutions to the original problem, e.g.:

- use a cat for get someone else to do the job
- use chocolate for develop a reward system
- use the boot for take a disciplined approach to learning, etc., etc.

Choose an object

Procedure 1 Identify the problem, e.g., 'How to motivate staff'.
2 Choose an object, e.g., a lamp, cup, coat hanger, etc.
3 List the attributes of the object. For example, in the case of the lamp:

- helps one to see
- flexible
- pretty, etc.

4 Relate the attributes to the original problem, e.g.:

- helps one to see for clarify their areas of responsibility
- flexible for encourage initiative
- pretty for positively reward initiative, etc., etc.

Figure 4.6   Creative problem solving techniques

Having described the above approaches, the trainer can then ask the team to choose a real problem that needs addressing. In terms of tackling this problem, in say 60 minutes, they will be asked to use one or more of the above techniques. They will also be asked to consciously use the group behaviours that aided creativity and to restrict the use of those that inhibited it.

If time permits, it is useful to provide the opportunity for the team to run one of their normal meetings as a way of attempting to integrate the learning (it may well be too early for them to incorporate their agreed proposals for the conduct of meetings, however). Therefore, prior to this part of the programme each member will be asked to contribute as at a normal meeting of the team, but, additionally, to consciously experiment with one of the behaviours described by Rackham (see p. 48) and pay attention to the behaviour of their colleagues. This exercise is best reviewed by each person in turn offering a statement about the success of their own experiments and to describe what they noticed. (This exercise also provides a good opportunity to use CCTV as part of the review process.)

Action planning and review

The final part of the programme should be concerned with the agreement of action plans and the kind of review process that will help the group continue the learning experience. In terms of the former, this will need to concentrate on individual action plans (to supplement the proposals for team meetings, which have already been agreed). In briefing team members, it is important to stress the need for realistic behavioural targets. Again, the categories Rackham describes are particularly useful in this respect. Experience would suggest that such plans are more likely to be achieved when individuals identify positive targets, e.g., 'I intend to use the summarizing behaviour at meetings'. The setting of negative targets, e.g., 'I must stop attacking/defending', seems only to work as a form of flagellation i.e.,—'There I go again'. The increased use of a positive behaviour target inexorably leads to a reduction of a negative pattern.

It is also advisable for these individual plans to be collected so that a collated list can be given to each member of the team. These working documents provide a structure for the review process. As suggested earlier (see p. 27, ff.), it should already have been agreed with the client and the team when a review will take place with the trainer. This review meeting, which can easily be held on-site, need take no longer than half a day and, at its simplest, should require no more than the team reporting their progress regarding their action plans.

Interventions by the trainer

The most appropriate intervention style for the trainer is that of being non-directive, i.e., encouraging the team to conduct their own analysis, diagnosis and strategy for development. During the course of the programme, they should be intervening less and less. The trainer needs to adopt a directive style, however, when managing the review sessions. The use of normal open-ended questions, e.g., 'What have you learnt from this activity?', can cause severe credibility problems with the team. A better choice would be to structure the review tightly. For example, ask the question of the team, 'What did you, and others do, that helped the team achieve the task?', then write down the answers on a flipchart.

With the principle that you only ask others to do what you are also prepared to do in mind, it is advisable for the trainer to offer feedback to individual team members in the group. The feedback, in keeping with the approach, should be *descriptive* only, i.e., describing observable behaviour (e.g., 'You were offering a suggestion at that stage'). Apart from the benefits of modelling appropriate feedback behaviour, you are also being perceived as sharing the same risk level.

The types of interventions to avoid—and discourage in others—are those that invite someone to pay attention to their feelings, encourage any speculation as to the underlying meaning of someone's behaviour or encourage any form of introspection, e.g., 'Why did you do that?'

Problems and how to handle them

The reason for the above injunction is that the major problem likely to arise is the emergence of a process issue—either historical (e.g., 'Remember what you said to me two years ago . . .') or current (e.g., 'I feel really depressed about what happened in that exercise'). When this occurs, a reminder of the ground rules may be enough to deflect the concern. If, however, the problem remains and becomes intrusive (i.e., interrupting the learning process), then it will need to be tackled head-on.

A good option for dealing with such an issue is to treat it as a problem that is likely to arise in teams. The intention is to depersonalize it as much as possible and to invite all members to engage in a problem-solving process. For example, by saying:

Bob has just said how he feels depressed about his contribution in that exercise. Given that this is a problem that we have or can all experience, what suggestions can we offer to help him learn from the experience?

The invitation by the trainer is to *think* about the situation with a view to offering practical support. The use of the group in this way is particularly pertinent to trying to deal with an open conflict between two members. Choosing to put them on one side while the group attempt to find an answer to the problem not only provides a salutary cooling-off period, but also makes everyone aware that this conflict is a *team* issue.

When this strategy does not work, and the problem continues to interfere with the learning process, the trainer is advised to say to the person(s) involved, 'I want to help you to deal with the situation and I would like to know what you want for yourself now?' The intention is to help the person discover some practical step for moving forward. In response to the question, the person may want to be left alone, be given time on their own, talk with just one member of the team, get some fresh air or whatever. If they choose to leave the room for any period of time, then the rejoining process needs to be explicitly managed. This may involve nothing more sophisticated than saying to the person when they return, 'Are you OK to continue?' Under these circumstances, there is often an assumption that if we ignore what is happening, then this is for the best. In practice, such avoidance creates a great deal of awkwardness for all parties.

The other potential problem with this approach is that the team is totally seduced by the tasks and they loose sight of the learning objectives. They then end up feeling bad about their continuing failure, e.g., 'There we go again'. Although this often starts as a joke, it can quickly degenerate into feelings of frustration and blame (the target for the latter may be themselves, particular individuals, the trainer or the choice of exercise). There is a danger, under these circumstances, that the normal cycle of activity and review merely feeds the spiral downwards. A better choice is to utilize the experience by asking that team members continue to fail, thus setting them a task and asking them to exaggerate their problem behaviours for that period. Such an opportunity helps groups to overcome the learning block. This is a variant of the 'Avoid Making a Decision' exercise (see p. 52).

Provided the programme structure is followed and feedback is limited to skills, then the risk level is relatively low and and the learning gains should be clearly identified.

Summary

In this chapter I have identified factors that point to using the task approach to team building. I have also described the key features of this approach and have offered some examples of the kinds of exercises and theory appropriate to such programmes. In conclusion, I have examined some of the issues that may face the trainer when using this approach.

References

1 Rackham, Neil, *Behaviour Analysis in Training.* McGraw-Hill, 1977.
2 Pfeiffer, J. William, (ed.) *The Encyclopedia of Team Building Activities,* 2 vols. San Diego: Pfeiffer & Company, 1991.
3 Woodcock, Mike, *50 Activities for Teambuilding.* Gower, 1989.

5 The group approach

Diagnostic factors

The group approach is primarily concerned with developing or maintaining a cohesive and integrated group. The particular behaviours to be identified and explained are:

- gatekeeping—ensuring that members who have a contribution to make are provided with the appropriate opportunity to do so
- encouraging—this also serves to keep the communication channels open
- harmonizing and compromising
- diagnosing, standard setting and testing—the recognition that problems arise in groups and that they need to be dealt with, either proactively, by agreeing ground rules, or reactively, by reviewing the process of the group.

Therefore, the learning goals associated with these behaviours include:

- understanding the distinction between content and process
- understanding group process, particularly stages of group development
- leadership and membership skills
- behaviour in groups, particularly the skills of influencing
- monitoring and reviewing the process of the team.

In undertaking the analysis and diagnosis, what will become apparent is that the problems of the team arise from the kind of 'task seduction' described in the last chapter (see p. 59). The leader and the group are well-intentioned, but the more they attempt to progress, the less they achieve. The kinds of teams that benefit from this approach include those shown in Figure 5.1.

- Management teams that have basic skills in team working, derived from management training.
- Management teams that have a history of working together to a reasonable level of effectiveness.
- Management teams that have neither an autocratic leader nor any major interpersonal skills conflicts.
- Teams the members of which are also likely to be involved as leaders and members of other teams.
- Teams that will be disbanded in the near future as a result of

organizational restructuring (the purpose in such cases is for individuals to take the learning from this team forward to their leadership and membership of new teams).

For project teams that have been given a responsibility for facilitating and/or managing organizational change.

Figure 5.1   *The types of teams—group*

For the majority of project teams this approach to team building is largely peripheral. The *raison d'etre* of most project teams is to complete a task to a fairly tight deadline. For a period of time, task seduction is likely to be functional if a trade-off is made in terms of some frustration at the individual level. Therefore, team building should only be contemplated if this level of frustration is seriously affecting both the members and the task. However, where such a team is charged with some responsibility of organizational change, then the *experience of a group process team building* should enlarge their understanding of the task that they are involved in delivering for the organization.

Similarly, I have been asked to offer these team building programmes as a precursor to organizational change. The function of such events are two-fold. First, to help teams come to terms with, and learn from the process of disbanding and separation. (It is interesting to note that, in organizational life, whereas organizations are beginning to take responsibility for *team building*, very few are yet aware of the painful and dysfunctional process involved in *team destruction*. The unfinished business this creates for individuals can quickly harden into resistance to any and all other organizational change). The second function of team building under these circumstances is to facilitate the movement from old to new teams by providing everyone with the skills and understanding of group process in general based on a review of their experiences within this team.

As will become apparent in this chapter, it is important to maintain a very strict boundary between *group* and *individual* process. Therefore, where team performance is severely handicapped by an extreme leadership style or conflict between individuals, this approach is not a good choice. Trying to maintain the boundary with such teams is extraordinarily difficult; the team find it difficult to let go of the issues and the trainer spends most of the time fire fighting.

Administration

Because of the higher risk level involved in this approach, a residential programme is the best choice. It provides the opportunity for individuals to continue the building process in the less-pressurized atmosphere of social contact out of hours. The kind of programme described in this chapter is designed for a team of between 6 and 15 members, with 1, but preferably 2 trainers, and to be run over 3 to 4 days. There is little flexibility with the parameter of group size: fewer than 6 members and there is not enough material; more than 15 and both the risk level and the amount of potential process is too much to cope with.

Methodology

The basic methodology of this approach is to increase the awareness of group process and the identification and practising of process skills. Because of the somewhat nebulous quality of process skills, as opposed to the more tangible task ones, it is important to inform all parties at the earliest opportunity of what will take place. The trainer needs to be aware that the legacy of sensitivity training—both the real and fantasy versions—have left in many organizations trace elements of fear and anger. An event such as this is likely to bring to the surface these feelings and concerns. One immediate method for dealing with this problem is to provide a detailed programme as soon as possible to allay fears. The structure of the programme—*particularly if it is in language they understand* (e.g., 'How groups work' rather than 'Group process')—will provide some certainties rather than mere rumour.

Preparatory work

For the same reason, the setting of preparatory work will help to provide some certainty, both about the existence of a structure and the level of risk that will be involved. The choice of a particular activity should be guided by two principles. The first is that they are being asked to think about the group rather than individual members. The second is that they are being asked, whether as a member or the leader, to begin to take some responsibility for the performance of the team.

Some examples of appropriate activities include the following.

- As a team we work best when . . .?
  As a team we get stuck when . . .?

- This team helps me by . . .
  I help this team by . . .

In both these cases, team members would be asked to consider these questions and bring their written answers to the event.

A third choice, which is both more demanding in terms of preparation and more revealing in terms of insight, is the following.

Explain, as to a Martian, the purposes of this team and how it works to achieve them. Assume that the Martian has no understanding of either teams or the need for people to work together.

Typically, in trying to formulate their explanations, team members are left with more questions than answers. Where they *are* able to provide explanations of what happens, they begin to question both the *whys* and the *hows*. What also surfaces when these explanations are shared is the wide disparity of understanding among team members. When briefing the group about this exercise, these particular reasons for choosing it should also be made clear.

This preparatory exercise is typical of the kind of activities that can be used for group approaches to teambuilding, i.e., creative and unusual. By contrast, such exercises would be highly unsuitable for either of the other two approaches. Both of them need a more pragmatic, down to earth mentality—in the case of the task approach, because it suits the rather prosaic subject matter; for the individual approach, the high risk level makes these creative exercises unsuitable.

Design features

In many ways, programmes using this approach are both more difficult to design and manage. At a positive level, there is far more choice available in the kinds of activities that can be used, e.g., substitute task and real; use of imagery and physical contact as vehicles for learning; questionnaires and discussions; theory, etc. This choice also enables the trainer to change the pace of the programme, e.g., from lengthy and serious decision making about future action to quick, creative exercises to explore the notions of boundaries (see the Boundaries exercises later in this chapter). This provides an opportunity, but also more danger of changing the pace inappropriately.

Some general features of design that help manage the risk include the following. First, start by using substitute activities to open up the process concepts, e.g., like the 'Martian' preparation exercise above, but aim to use real tasks as soon as possible. Substitute tasks can then be reintroduced merely to change the pace. (As a rough guide, overall, use 30 per cent substitute tasks to 70 per cent real. This is a straightforward reversal of the desired proportions for task approaches.)

This approach will mesh with the second design feature—starting at the general level, e.g., the notion of roles in a group, then moving to the particular, e.g., who does what in this group?

Although these features both contribute to a gradual raising of the risk level, it is the management of two other boundaries by the trainer that are the most crucial.

The first of these boundaries is the time frame of the activities, i.e., there and then, or, here and now. It is far wiser to ask teams to learn from what they have *done* (last year, last week, 10 minutes ago)—there and then—than from what they are *doing*—the here and now. The former has moved away from the immediacy of the experience and provides them, where required, with opportunities to rationalize, avoid or deflect from the learning. It provides an important escape route to maintain face, e.g., 'I'm not normally like that'. By paying attention to what is happening now as a vehicle for learning, all escape routes will have to be dramatic, e.g., 'I have had enough of this. I'm going'.

The second boundary is that between thinking and feeling. Because the learning is focused on group process rather than skills, the emotional concerns about leadership and membership, roles, inclusion and exclusion, can intrude powerfully into even a conceptual learning activity. For example, on the receiving end of a theory input on stages of group development, individuals are suddenly able to give a reason for, or explanation of, vague emotions that they had previously deemed unimportant. To minimize the dangers of this kind of intrusion, the selection of and briefing for activities should emphasize the need for thinking and problem solving. In addition, the trainer will need to avoid the use of that intervention sacred to all management programmes, 'How are you feeling?' In most cases, this elicits a thinking process. Luckily, many trainers who ask this question have a similar inability to discriminate. There is a severe danger, however, that, for once, it might produce a statement about feelings. Such a statement, once solicited, would then have to be dealt with.

For the same reason, try to introduce all the group process concepts as early as possible and try to ensure that, in the last half day, if not longer, the activities should be heavily based on problem solving or decision making. (If the boundary between thinking and feeling is to be disrupted, give everyone as much time as possible to resolve the issues).

The ground rules The introductory activities should be largely concerned with creating the right climate for the team and beginning to establish a relationship between the trainer and the team. The role of the trainer is much more of an issue with group approaches. The traditional management trainer role, appropriate for task approaches, gives way to the more nebulous function of facilitator. It is also likely that members of the team could well raise the matter of the nature of this relationship during the course of the event, and this can take any form from 'What do you think?' to 'Why do we need you?'

The level of anxiety is also likely to be high, so the choice of introductions should allow opportunities to discharge some of these feelings. Use of the standard 'Hopes, fears and expectations' introduction as follows:

- my best hope for this event . . .
- my worst fear . . .
- my reasonable expectation . . .

can provide this outlet. However, if there is a lot of anxiety around, this format can encourage the opposite of what is desired. In these situations a better choice would be:

- what I would like us to achieve by the end is . . .
- the major obstacle to achieving this is . . .
- what I can do to deal with the obstacle is . . .

This latter format provides an opportunity to discharge the feelings, but immediately encourages individuals to take a problem solving approach to managing the situation for themselves.

These statements should be logged on a flipchart and used as a precursor to setting the ground rules. These would include:

- confidentiality (see p. 47)
- the aims of the event are:

  —to develop their understanding of the process that teams experience
  —to provide the skills to diagnose and deal with the problems that arise in teams
  —to provide them with an opportunity to review the functions and practises of this team

- the role of the trainer is to provide structure, guidance, theory and feedback to help the team reach their decisions
- the role of the group (see p. 47)
- the normal rules for giving feedback will apply:

  —for the giver to:
    check that your feedback is required by the receiver
    address the person directly
    offer your feedback as information
    check that the receiver has had enough
  —for the receiver to:
    accept the feedback as information
    ask for clarification where necessary
    decide how to use the information

- in addition to feedback, the learning approach will include theory, discussions and activities
- the team will be asked to agree decisions about their future operation.
- the role of the trainer will be to facilitate these discussions.

The concerns that have been recorded on the board from the introductory activities should then be reviewed with a view to adding to the list of ground rules.

One additional ground rule worth adding *after* this process is the following:

- the above ground rules can be added to and/or reviewed at any stage during this event.

The rules should then be posted on flipchart paper in a prominent place within the room. Some of the sessions e.g., leadership/membership, stages of group development are likely to give rise to such reviews.

The exercises and theory

Group behaviours

Before starting the preparatory work, it is advisable to offer a model of team effectiveness. Because it is a process approach, it makes more sense to use the Schein model than it does the Adair model. The theory input would be an abridged version of the description given in Chapter 3 (see p. 34, ff.) and centre on Figure 3.3. In describing the three basic needs that have to be met by an effective team, it is useful to give examples of the behaviours associated with each need.

As a way of accommodating the preparatory work, it is helpful to describe the process symptoms (see p. 36–7, ff.) that arise when teams are seduced by the task. Not only does it help them to understand the model, but it also legitimizes their concerns about the team. By asking each member in turn to read out their comments on the team and asking the rest of the team *not to comment on the concerns*, but, instead, to assign it to one of the three areas—task, group or individual—what should emerge is a confirmation of the trainer's diagnosis of the team, i.e., the concerns should be primarily concerned with the group process. Any stray issues that fall into either of the other two areas should be dealt with, but only when the more substantial issues have been addressed. This activity should also vindicate the content of the programme.

Before dealing with these issues, it is a good investment to offer a behaviour framework for the team and a modified version of the Schein categories, shown in Figure 5.2, is appropriate.[1]

Each behaviour by a group member can be interpreted as being *primarily* directed towards one of the following: achieving the *task*, building or maintaining a cohesive *group*, or expressing *individual* needs and interests.

Task behaviour includes:

- making suggestions, defining problems
- seeking or giving information
- clarifying, interpreting or summarizing ideas
- seeking or taking decisions.

Group behaviour includes:

- reconciling differences between group members
- reducing tension through humour
- keeping communication channels open
- modifying personal views in the interests of group cohesion.

Individual behaviour includes:

- openly expressing needs and interests
- dominating others, being aggressive or blocking

- seeking help or recognition through self-deprecation, personal confusion or not listening
- pairing up and forming subgroups
- withdrawing.

Observation roles

1 List each behaviour exhibited by your subject in the respective category, so that, at the end of the exercise, the total number of contributions can be recorded.
2 Try also to make a note of some examples of these behaviours in each category and evaluate the effect of the behaviours on others in the group.

Figure 5.2 · Schein behaviour categories

With this framework, there is clearly an option to move away from the purely quantitative to the qualitative approach—observers are being asked to interpret and evaluate the effects of the behaviour. To familiarize people with this framework, the ideal method is to run two 'fishbowl' activities, with half the group observing the others. To ensure a clearer understanding of the categories, the choice of substitute tasks is helpful. Two contrasting, but appropriate tasks, would be a decision-making exercise and a problem-solving task. First, the decision-making task.

Priorities

Briefing

> This group has 25 minutes to agree, and rank in priority order, the 10 most important politicians (films, songs, pop groups etc.) since 1945.

Now the problem-solving task.

Board game

Briefing

> This group has 25 minutes to design and construct a new board game for adults.

Where it is possible to run two such activities with one-on-one feedback, it is worth ensuring that pairs (a subject and an observer in each) change roles for the second exercise. There is no advantage in inadvertently creating a competitive element in the feedback process.

Most groups will need some time before they become proficient in the use of these categories, so it is important that all are given permission *not* to be expert through these exercises. In addition, this is a model that can be used again during the programme and each member of the team will be requested to reflect on their continuing contributions to the team in terms of this model. Even at this stage, it is worth encouraging them all to consciously experiment with their behaviour in future activities, e.g., someone who scores high in task behaviours can experiment with the use of more group behaviours. As this provides a useful framework for the individual action planning at the end of the programme, such experimentation would accelerate the particular learning process.

The diagnosis will have determined both the choice of topics and their respective emphases in the programme. What follows is an outline of a programme designed to develop any team's awareness and skills in group process. This outline also attempts to show the range of activities that can be used. The topics to be covered here are content and process, stages of group development and boundaries, roles in teams, motivation and the concept of 'strokes', plus the development of ground rules.

Content and process

This intervention is particularly important for teams that are heavily seduced by the task. The theoretical input can be adequately covered by the following.

When looking at communication between people, it is possible to identify two different levels occurring at the same time:

- the *content*—the literal meaning of the words used by the speaker,
- the *process*—the way in which the words are delivered.

This is sometimes referred to as the words (content) and the music (process). The process level is conveyed by means of the whole range of non-verbal behaviour (facial expressions, tone of voice, gesture, posture, eye contact, physical proximity, etc.). All of these non-verbal behaviours convey a lot of clues to our feelings and attitudes about ourselves and those to whom we are talking. Much of the time, the process matches the content, e.g., 'I am sad' is said in a slow, heavy voice with eyes looking downward, by a speaker with tears in their eyes and a catch in their voice. Under such circumstances, the message is clear and unambiguous to the listener. However, there are also a number of times when there is a mismatch between the content and the process. There are certain phrases and formulae in common use that are intended to 'tone down' or 'distort' the true message. For example:

- 'I'm sorry, but . . .' when the person is not at all sorry
- 'We'll come back to that later . . .' when the person has no idea about the topic
- 'Oh, . . . I see' when the person has no idea what you are talking about
- 'Yes . . ., but . . .' when the person means 'No!'

- 'With all due respect . . .' when the person means 'That is rubbish, but I don't want to offend you'
- 'Are you sure about that?' when the person is not sure themselves
- 'Why did you do it that way?' when the person thinks you have got it wrong
- 'Did you check with anyone else?' when the person thinks you should have asked them
- 'I would love to agree with you' when the person will enjoy resisting the invitation to do so.

In each case, we infer the unspoken process meaning that follows what is said above by means of some significant non-verbal behaviours, e.g., the slow, triumphant smile, the averted eyes, the posture of aggression, etc. The outcome of the communication, and the state of the relationship, will be largely determined by what happens at this process level. For example, the verbal exchanges may appear polite and amicable, but both parties have withdrawn from the exchange, awaiting the opportunity to renew hostilities. Often we are aware of both our own process messages and those of others. However, there are times when self-awareness is blocked and we do not see the other person bridle at our comments. These blockages of awareness are very common in teams because individual exchanges are overlooked or ignored in pursuit of the task. However, the bad feelings remain. They can be disguised and discharged in other ways, e.g., through the use of put-down humour that becomes the main currency of communication in a group.

One vehicle for exploring this concept is the 'Personal patterns' exercise.

Personal patterns

Briefing

1 Individually, think about your experiences of being a member of this team. At a typical meeting, what kinds of thoughts and feelings do you experience on a regular basis? In the light of what you know about yourself, what clues or patterns of non-verbal behaviours do you imagine you show to others?
2 Now think about each of your colleagues. What patterns of non-verbal behaviours have you noticed each of them display? For each, describe what you have noticed and try to interpret an underlying meaning for the pattern.
3 Share and compare your answers with three or four colleagues.
4 In large groups, report back on your findings.

Notes   Although this is a high-risk, self-disclosure and feedback exercise, the fact that it is used to explore a concept and is initially worked through in small groups, means that the level is manageable. By asking people to reveal clues about when they are finding it difficult to express—which is really what this exercise pays attention to—means that the team now have an early warning system to prevent the unfinished business simply collecting. This provides an opportunity for examining group process.

Stages of group development

Having developed an understanding of process at the individual level, the wider picture for their experiences, that of being a member of this team, is provided by an input on stages of group development (see p. 38–40, ff.). The question that immediately arises from the presentation is 'What do you perceive to be our stage?'

In refusing to answer the question, the trainer can use this natural curiosity as the basis for an exercise in which the team determine their own answer and have the opportunity to identify practical steps for their progression. To this end, a small input on boundaries (see p. 64, ff.) provides them with the diagnostic toolkit for the following exercise.

Boundaries 1

Briefing

> 1 In small groups (threes or fours), using the description provided, agree which stage of development you think that this team has reached.
> 2 In terms of improving effectiveness, first, what, in your judgement, are the key boundaries that need to be addressed and, second, what specific actions are required by members of this team?

Notes

When the small groups return to share their findings, they are involved in the development of an embryonic action plan for the team. Therefore, it is worth keeping their conclusions on flipchart paper to revisit later on in the event.

As mentioned at the beginning of this chapter, one of the more creative activities can be used as an alternative to this exercise. As this activity involves physical contact—one of the really important boundaries in any group—the trainer should only use it with carefully selected groups, e.g., teams of management trainers.

Boundaries 2

Briefing

> In pairs, sit on the floor with a cushion between you. This cushion represents an important boundary in your relationship as members of this team, e.g., openness, honesty, friendship, cooperation.
>
> Having agreed the nature of the boundary, you have five minutes to find as many ways as possible for physically managing the boundary of the cushion.
>
> At the end of the five minutes, you will be asked to report on the actions that you discovered.

Notes   At the end of the five minutes, all these actions are listed on the board (e.g., one person walking across the cushion, both people joining hands across the cushion, both standing up, each holding a corner of the cushion, one person throwing the cushion away, etc.). The exercise illustrates the repertoire of choices for managing the real boundary and each pair will be asked to choose one of the physical options that they tried and relate it to the real boundary between them. Because the exercise involves 'acting out' the issue as well as the clear possibility of physical contact, the trainer needs to be acutely aware of the possibility that some unfinished business may emerge for the individual. This unfinished business may have nothing to do with the matter in hand, i.e., the relationship with the other person, but could well stem from a powerful historical episode.

The positive benefits of this exercise are that it helps to make the important concept of boundaries very clear and it is useful as a practical diagnostic tool.

Roles in teams

As mentioned in Chapter 3, one of the most common approaches used to address the concept of roles is that of the Belbin model.[2] However, because of the reservations that were also expressed there about its practical application on a team building programme (see p. 32–3), a trainer may wish to consider alternatives. One exercise I have used adopts the analogy most often used by team members, i.e., the sports team, to open up the analysis. The particular model I have used is as follows.

The football team

Briefing

Individually, think about the roles that you and the others play in the team. To help you in your analysis, think of the kinds of roles that can be found in a soccer team. The more common ones are as follows:

- *goalkeeper* the last line of defence; the team rely on them to take command in a crisis
- *fullback* also plays a defensive, steady role, but is capable of picking up a new idea and running with it; usually leaves the star contributions to other members of the team
- *defenders* unspectacular members of the team; do a steady job; team could not function without them but they are often unappreciated
- *sweeper* major role is to anticipate problems and to keep calm under pressure; offers support to all members of the team and plays a very steady game
- *midfield maestro* creative member of the team with lots of ideas and imagination; can overextend themselves and the team by being too demanding
- *strikers* key members of the team, responsible for achieving targets; need to work well together, but can get in each others' way
- *captain* primary role is to make sure the team works effectively; seems to have the ability to motivate each member of the team
- *referee* recognized authority on how to play the game effectively; the team rely on them for guidance and information.

Which of these roles most closely describes you, and which role would you ascribe to each of your colleagues? If it helps you to modify these definitions or if, in your judgement, a particular member of the team displays characteristics of different roles then show this in your answer.

Notes

At the end of 20 minutes on their own, team members are asked to log their answers on flipchart paper. My experience of using this exercise is that there is a remarkable similarity of perceptions. What is really important, however, is the discussion that follows about the roles that individuals play as team members. To build on this concept of roles, it is useful to follow the discussion with another group exercise *in which team members are asked to experiment with another role*, e.g., a midfield maestro moves into defence for one game.

Obviously, any organized game is capable of being used for this purpose, nor does the trainer need to even offer rudimentary descriptions of roles—these can be generated by the group.

The particular advantages of this exercise, though, are first, that the categories and their definitions are unimportant and not to be taken too seriously by trainers or course members, second, that they relate to most people's experiences of teams and, third, they engage the creativity of most groups. If a trainer wishes to use Belbin, or something similar, it is worth encouraging team members to experiment, if only once, by consciously trying other roles. Without such an opportunity, the danger is that people are left with the impression that, having been defined as belonging to a category, they are now fixed in that role for all time. Obviously, such a view is the antithesis of all developmental training.

Leadership and membership

What normally flows from a consideration of roles is the broad distinction between the roles of *leader* and *members*. Obviously one stimulus in this area is to offer theory on the nature of leadership and, clearly, there is a wealth of information available. A better option is to invite the team to clarify both the roles and responsibilities that they would see as being appropriate for their needs. The simplest method for this is to split the team into two and brief each as follows:

Roles and responsibilities

Briefing

> Each group has 20 minutes to list on a flipchart:
>
> • the roles and responsibilities of the leader
> • the roles and responsibilities of the members.

Notes

The team is split at random—the leader could go into either group and the final list is drawn up as a result of negotiations between the two groups *and not between the leader and the members*. (To split into the latter can lead to polarization between two power blocks.)

As an addition to their own conclusions, the list shown in Figure 5.3 can be usefully offered by the trainer.

1 Listen to the content and the process.
2 Be aware of the frequency and distribution of comments.
3 Be aware of non-verbal behaviour.
4 Watch out for the development of subgroups.
5 Summarize periodically.
6 Be aware of unexpressed conflict.
7 Be willing to ask for and give feedback to each other.
8 Do not put down yourself or others, either implicitly or explicitly.
9 Check your assumptions and inferences.
10 Be prepared to initiate as well as respond.
11 Pay attention to examples of the following behaviours:

- withdrawal
- scapegoating
- sycophancy.

Figure 5.3 *Check-list of group leadership and membership skills*

The above skills are seen as being applicable to both members and leaders and this implies a model of team leadership that is primarily concerned with managing the *process* rather than the *task*.

Influencing

Although it is possible to look at the wider process of influencing, my experience of team building is that to do so would be to deflect from the immediate task, that is, development of the understanding and skills of group process. Within this context, however, it is possible to, first, offer some general guidelines on influencing in a group and, second, to pick up on the important aspect of offering recognition as a form of influence.

Influencing in groups is different in a number of ways to influencing on a one-to-one basis. Some of the main differences are as follows.

- *Third-party presence and involvement* Whatever happens between two individuals may have an impact on other members of the team as they will be observing and making judgements about the behaviours of the two people. Therefore, if something of contention takes place, it is always advisable to make an opportunity for the rest of the team to offer not only their judgements, but also their feelings. Denied that opportunity, the observers could well allow the experience to affect how open they will be to future influence by the characters involved.
- *Risk level* Given the number of people involved in any team, the sense of risk level is likely to be higher than for any one relationship. The factors that cause this are not merely the product of numbers, but the increased uncertainty and lack of control for the individual. There-fore, individuals in teams are likely to operate with a more limited repertoire of behaviour than they do outside the meeting.
- *Discrimination* Because an individual is responding to and involved with a range of individuals, it is fairly common, particularly when under pressure, not to discriminate, e.g., 'Everyone is against my idea!' This lack of discrimination is likely to be self-fulfilling! Therefore, it is important, moment by moment, to pay attention to the differences of behaviour among the individuals.
- *Climate* It is also important to be aware of the climate within a team. Good task suggestions and ideas are likely to be lost if there is some unresolved process issue just below the surface. Equally, not picking up the cues that a process intervention is likely to be seen by the group as a major distraction to an overwhelming need to move the task on, is another failure to read the climate.
- *Timing* Both in terms of when to raise issues and how much time an

individual is 'allowed' to contribute will affect an individual's capacity to influence. As a general observation, individuals deemed to be influential in a team are usually not those who talk at length, nor those with the most cogent arguments, but those who read the climate and pick their time effectively.

The offering or, more usually, the withholding, of recognition in a group is a major determinant of group process. The general complaint in most organizations is 'You are only told when you do a bad job—doing well is taken for granted' and it holds true for teams, too. More often, recognition is limited to non-verbal sounds and gestures of agreement. This process is a disincentive to both risk-taking and creativity.

My experience is that the simplest way to positively affect the process of a team is to develop an awareness, and hence an improvement in, the giving and receiving of recognition. One useful exercise for achieving this is the following.

Giving and receiving recognition

Briefing

> Individually, reflect on your experiences as a member of the team. First, identify some recent examples of you:
>
> • offering an explicit appreciation of someone else's contribution, e.g., saying, 'I like your idea'
> • offering an explicit condemnation, e.g., saying 'What a stupid suggestion'
> • wanting to do the first or second but not doing so.
>
> Second, think of recent occasions when you received an appreciation and/or condemnation of your contributions.

Notes   Having completed the individual work, the team are asked to share their answers and to then reflect on the particular profile of recognition that exists within the group. As a typical profile, what tends to emerge is little in the way of positive recognition, a greater incidence of negative recognition and a lot of implicit recognition, i.e., through the range of non-verbal behaviour. Based on their own analysis, the team can agree specific plans to change the pattern within their overall action plan.

A useful theory input to support this last activity would be that of the concept of 'strokes', which is part of the theory of Transactional Analysis.[3] The term 'stroke' is used to refer to a unit of recognition and the basic premise is that the giving and receiving of recognition is a basic and continuing need. This need, in its own way, being as important as the more obvious needs for oxygen, food, drink, etc. The options for giving and receiving strokes are shown in Figure 5.4.

	Verbal	*Non-verbal*
Positive for being	'I like you.'	Arm round the shoulder.
Positive for doing	'Thanks, for the help'.	A smile.
Negative for doing	'What a stupid idea!'	A frown.
Negative for being	'Get lost.'	Avoid eye contact.
No strokes	Silence.	Do not acknowledge.

Figure 5.4 *Strokes*

In terms of these options, it is suggested that, if we are in a situation where there is limited availability of positive strokes, then we will actively look for negative ones. The reason for this behaviour is that negative strokes are better than no strokes at all. This pattern is often evident in teams of men, where the unrelenting pattern of recognition is the remorseless exchange of put-downs. When confronted about this pattern, such teams will publicly declare this to be a friendly custom. In private, however, individuals are likely to complain about this part of their culture.

The reason offered for this by Transactional Analysis is contained in the concept of 'stroke economy'. This concept suggests that society appears to be based on some important rules about the exchange of strokes. These rules are shown in Figure 5.5.

1 Do not give positive strokes freely.
2 Never give physical strokes.
3 If you do give positive strokes, only give conditional ones.
4 Do not miss an opportunity to give negative strokes.
5 Do not ask for positive strokes—certainly not directly.
6 Do not give yourself positive strokes.
7 Never refuse insincere strokes.

Figure 5.5 *Stroke economy*

Although this provides a powerful stimulus for teams to review their working climate—in both presenting the theory and the choice of exercise—the trainer needs to ensure that the team stays focused at the group level. Any encouragement to pursue this concept at the individual or team relationships level is capable of moving into much riskier areas for all concerned.

Reviewing the process

As a bridge towards the final activity of action planning and as a way of closing down the process into the more appropriate thinking activities required, the team can be offered the opportunity to review how they are feeling about the team. Although this activity is best offered as a chance to be creative and have fun, the more serious purpose of it is to provide a safety valve for any unfinished business. The exercise is deceptively simple.

Draw a picture

Briefing

Each member of the team is to take a sheet of flipchart paper and pens and draw a picture that represents how they see the team. Although artistic skill is purely optional, do take time to find the right image to convey the view held.

Notes

When the pictures have been completed, the team members are brought back together and each person takes it in turn to describe their picture. The rest of the group are limited to asking individual questions for clarification only. If there are no problems, this activity provides an opportunity to discharge their good feelings about the event and the team. If there *are* problems, it provides an opportunity for dealing with them (see Problems and how to handle them below).

Action planning and review

Because of the wide range of activities covered on this kind of programme, it is important that at least half a day is devoted to the action planning. Some of the elements required to be brought together, e.g., individual experiments with Schein behaviour categories and non-verbal patterns of behaviour, the boundaries exercises, the team roles and individual stroke exercises, need time to be integrated into individual action plans.

When individuals have worked these different elements through to their own satisfaction, then it is advisable to bring them together to listen to the plans of all their colleagues. This can then be supplemented by written copies being made available to all members after the event.

At a team level, the starting point for the action plans will be the roles and responsibilities of members and leader that were negotiated during the programme. A useful vehicle for the team action planning is to ask them to agree, based on their experiences of the programme, a list of ground rules for their meetings back at work. An important constraint for this activity is that the list has to be intelligible for future members of the team, so all jargon is to be avoided. A written copy of the completed list is also to be made available to all after the event.

The review meeting—about six months after the event—should be held off-site and one day should be allocated to reviewing both the individual and team action plans.

Interventions by the trainer

The primary role is that of facilitator, i.e., encouraging and helping to expedite actions and decisions by the group. If the analysis and diagnosis are accurate, then the relevant areas, and their respective weightings on the programme, should be easy to assess. However, in the event, the programme will need to be far more flexible than would a task-based approach, so it is advisable that the trainer takes a number of options in terms of both theories and activities.

Such is the nature of group process, however, that it is foolish to pretend that the control or sequencing is truly within the control of the *trainer*. If particular problems surface at any stage, time will be required to resolve them. For example, it could well emerge while examining the roles within the team that there is a serious imbalance, e.g., they are all defenders and there are no strikers. To pursue the implications of this, and to identify future action for resolving the problem, may involve leaving out the part of the programme looking at the process of influence.

There is always a seductive component in a group process-based event that entices the trainer to 'go with the flow' (i.e., to go for the easy option of abdicating responsibility for learning in favour of simply feeling good). This temptation needs to be resisted because feeling happy about being a member of a team is a poor substitute for the team learning.

Problems and how to handle them

There are two major problems with this approach to team building. The first has already been alluded to above, i.e., feeling good and not learning. In the same way that teams can be seduced by the task, the process also has its attractions. As the team begins to push out its boundaries of trust, openness and risk-taking, it can begin to 'overheat' emotionally. Unfortunately, the first symptom of this happening is that the programme suddenly picks up dramatically: resistance, is replaced by excitement, which is one of the features that makes it attractive to trainers. The second symptom is that the team becomes remarkably tolerant and accepting of all and sundry, i.e., they uncritically accept *all* concepts and exercises. The individuals also feel remarkably happy about themselves and their colleagues and want to keep working for long hours in this environment. As they are not taking care of themselves, physically and emotionally, the 'hot house' team will burn out.

If the trainer picks up the signs and does not get hooked into the process, a good approach to the problem is to give them, first, a problem-solving activity (if necessary, bringing forward part of the action planning) or, second, a break from the programme with a recommendation that they spend some time on their own thinking about what they have learned.

The second major problem that can arise with this approach is a conflict between the trainer and the team. This is likely to arise because, in examining one of the most important boundaries in any team, i.e., membership, it can bring to the surface the role that the *trainer* has with the team. Some individuals might perceive this as being too influential, e.g., 'This is *our* team, not *yours*!' Others might start by making too many demands on a trainer and then resent their own dependency. If the trainer has any suspicion that there is a problem with the relationship, it is important to raise the concern as soon as possible. Some of the signs that this might be happening include sharp and increasing challenges of any or all comments, criticisms of presentations or briefings, lack of contributions and or energy in the training room or a perceptible change of climate when the trainer joins the group socially.

When this occurs, the resolution is likely to be uncomfortable and painful for the trainer. However, it is important that they take a problem-solving approach to renegotiating the relationship. To do this, it is important to request that each person in turn states, first, what they require from the trainer and, second, what they are prepared to offer. The trainer must also make clear their own requirements of, and offers to, the team.

Teams that have spent a lot of time either in the stages of dependency or counterdependency can take the safe opportunity of rehearsing with the trainer the process issues they need to manage within their own boundaries. For them, taking on the trainer is a safe rehearsal.

Summary

In this chapter, I have identified factors that point to using the group approach to team building. I have also described the key features of this approach and have offered some examples of the kinds of exercises and theory appropriate to such programmes. In conclusion, I have examined some of the issues that may face the trainer when using this approach.

References

1 Schein, Edgar, *Process Consultation* (2nd ed.) 2 vols. Addison-Wesley, 1988.
2 Belbin, Dr R.M., *Management Teams: Why They Succeed or Fail*. Heinemann, 1981.
3 Biddle, Derek, and Evenden, Robin, *Human Aspects of Management*. Institute of Personnel Management, 1980. (Chapter 4 provides a brief explanation of the main concepts of Transactional Analysis.)

6 The individual approach

Diagnostic factors

The individual approach is primarily concerned with how individuals bring personal needs for recognition, involvement, support and friendship to their membership of any team. When these needs are unfulfilled or blocked, then the following behaviours are likely to appear:

- dominating others, being aggressive or blocking the contribution of others
- seeking help or recognition through self-deprecation, personal confusion or not listening
- pairing up or forming subgroups or alliances for support or protection
- withdrawal—psychologically or physically.

Therefore, the learning goals associated with this approach include:

- awareness of their own behaviours and feelings moment by moment
- awareness of the behaviours and likely feelings of others moment by moment
- improvement of the skills of observation, interpretation and listening
- developing skills in self-expression and self-confidence
- skills of giving and receiving feedback
- understanding the processes of individual and organizational change
- developing strategies for changing organizational culture.

What should be clear during the stages of analysis and diagnosis is that the performance of the team is affected by the poor quality of relationships and personal communication. Any attempt to develop task skills or skills in managing group process would be sabotaged by the unfinished business between team members. In terms of meeting these learning goals, the focus is the nature and quality of the relationship between the individual and other members of the team. The kinds of teams that would benefit from this approach include those shown in Figure 6.1.

- Senior management teams that are likely to decree that team building is required by teams below them in the hierarchy.
- Teams (management or project) that have a major responsibility for diagnosing, implementing and reviewing organizational change strategies.

- Well-established teams with a history of drama or conflict.
- Teams where the leader has a desire to change their management style.
- Teams whose performance is handicapped by unfinished business and unresolved conflicts.
- Teams of management trainers who will provide facilitators for team building events for managers.

Figure 6.1   *The types of teams—individual*

All the types of teams listed in Figure 6.1 could be separated into two clear categories: remedial and developmental. In terms of the former, it might appear self-evident that all teams with major interpersonal problems or conflicts would automatically qualify for a team building event. However, not all these types of problems are suitable for or appropriate to this kind of intervention. Although the purpose of this approach to team building is to change the behaviours and attitudes of individuals, it does require a certain amount of willingness on their part before the operation can be seriously considered. Equally clearly, the trainer will discover problems where a willingness to change is demonstrably absent. In these cases, a managerial intervention, e.g., disciplinary action, is more appropriate. One of the key tasks facing the trainer during the analysis and diagnosis is that of making judgements about what is possible. Characteristically, the problem individual will attempt to foreclose on the preparatory interview by declaring, 'I approach this event with an open mind'. In such cases, the underlying meaning of such a phrase is likely to be somewhere along the spectrum from 'I will need to be persuaded' to 'Over my dead body' to 'I will not permit anyone else to learn.'

On interpersonal skills programmes, such statements are not only common, but are often non-negotiable, i.e., the person saying this is sitting in the learning group. Because of the structure of most programmes— moving from low risk to high—such people can be left alone for a period and can also be managed effectively by the group. On team building, however, these options are not available (see Design features, later in this chapter). When encountering this, the trainer is better advised to confront the underlying process. For example, by saying 'I do not believe you—I think that you are unwilling to learn'. For many trainers this intervention may appear unnecessarily confrontational and outside the scope of their normal repertoire. The real choice, unfortunately, is not whether or not to confront, but where (the interview or the event).

The trainer may be asked to accept this kind of individual by both the leader and the team, with everyone hoping for a dramatic conversion of Damascus proportions. If the trainer feels that there is no option but to take such an individual on the event, it is worth, first, expressing your perception of this person's 'openness' and, second, demanding of that individual a clear contract that they will not attempt to undermine the learning of the others. Without the contract, the trainer is likely to have their attention diverted during the event, awaiting the sabotage.

Similarly, it is possible that a particular team can be so full of unfinished business that the prospect of a useful intervention is slight. A more appropriate choice would be to re-form the membership at the earliest opportunity. Although this might appear to be a negative response, both the trainer and the client need to be aware of the consequences of taking on such a challenge—and failing!

In general terms, team building programmes that fall into the developmental category are likely to have less in the way of deep, unfinished business between individuals than others. What often compensates for this lack of conflict *between* individuals is the unresolved conflict *within* individuals, particularly in the area of lack of self-confidence. My experience of working with teams charged with managing organizational change is that a major obstacle to team effectiveness is the competitive process engendered by this self-doubt. The surfacing of this issue in an individual is often accompanied by a lot of emotion.

Administration

Without a doubt, the best choice for this kind of event is a residential programme of three to four days. This provides everyone with an opportunity to talk through and clarify any misunderstandings that are likely to arise. It is not uncommon, for instance, for an individual to happily accept a piece of feedback that, on reflection, causes them problems. The programme described in this chapter is designed for a team of between 6 and 12 members, run by 2 trainers. It is possible to include up to 16 people, but it means that the trainers have to take and maintain a highly directive and controlling approach. This directive approach means that the trainers are often listening intently for hours at a stretch, so having two provides some safety net against any loss of attention. However, the trainers need to be in complete accord about their respective roles and responsibilities, otherwise their differences will distract the team from its main purpose.

Methodology

The basic methodology of this approach is the development of personal awareness. Although the initial focus is on the relationships within the group, the exchange of feedback serves two separate, but interrelated, purposes. First, feedback provides an opportunity to clear up unfinished business between members as a precursor to clarifying the group process and dealing with strategic issues. Second, the feedback provides individuals with information that is applicable to all their relationships.

It is important that the feedback is not seen as an end in itself—it is intended to develop an awareness of individual behaviour in a group as well as an opportunity to practice giving and receiving feedback. If these aspects of the methodology are not picked up by the trainer as explicit learning points, the danger is that the value of the event is marginalized to being no more than a 'team service', akin to servicing a car.

This approach to team building is based upon the learning cycle shown in Figure 6.2.

- *Awareness* Paying attention to behaviour and feelings moment by moment with a view to assessing effectiveness in terms of meeting my needs without adversely affecting my relationships.
- *Choices* Once I am aware of what I do at this moment, I am also able to identify the range of other choices available. For example, if I am aware that, though I feel frustrated, I am sitting doing nothing, other choices would involve me doing something, e.g., screaming, shouting, stating feelings, making a request, etc., etc.
- *Experiments* The next stage is to try one of these choices, e.g., make a request, and then experience the consequences for myself and others.
- *Decisions* Having tried other choices and received feedback, I am now in a good position to make decisions about my future use of these behaviours.

Figure 6.2   Process learning model

The individual patterns of behaviour that will be identified as obstacles for individuals on team building programmes are just as likely to be unproductive not only in other teams, but in relationships generally. For example, not expressing my frustration or acting on it positively in a one-to-one relationship is likely to be equally unproductive for myself and the other person.

Preparatory work

For this approach, some form of preparatory work is highly recommended. The aims of such work are as much to do with managing the process as they are to do with having prepared content. The key process aim of the activity is to encourage each person to think through the risk levels of their own answers and to anticipate what might be offered them by their colleagues. In providing this opportunity, individuals are likely to have moments of discomfort in anticipation, but this is preferable to them experiencing the sharp increase of risk attendant on being asked to do something similar without the preparation. In being asked to prepare beforehand, each person has the opportunity to consider the risk level that they wish to work at without the immediate influence of peer pressure.

There are a number of choices available for this kind of activity. Some examples follow:

- Three problems/concerns I have as a member of this team are . . .
- My thoughts about being a member of this team are . . .
  My feelings about being a member of this team are . . .
- What I like about each of my colleagues is . . .
  What I dislike about each of my colleagues is . . .

Any activity that provides an opportunity for each member to express their concerns, needs or feelings, is appropriate. My personal choice is the following role negotiation exercise because, first, each member is required to address every other member, second, it provides a framework for a balance between positive and negative feedback and, third, each person is asked to focus on what *can* be changed. The written briefing shown in Figure 6.3 is given and directly explained to each member at the stage of analysis and diagnosis.

Preparation   Some three or four weeks before the team building event, reflect on the daily experiences of doing your job. Consider also, the number and nature of your dealings with colleagues, both at team meetings and outside.

In terms of, first, improving your effectiveness and, second, improving your level of satisfaction, write down, for each member of the team, the statements you wish to make to them under the following headings:

- I would like you to do more of . . .
- I would like you to do less of . . .
- I would like you to continue doing . . .

The nature of each statement could be to do with your *relationship*, e.g., 'I would like you to demonstrably listen to me' or may be to do with their *behaviour* at team meetings, e.g., 'I would like you to be more open to the ideas of others' or may be to do with work *procedures*, e.g., 'I would like you to continue delegating responsibility to me'.

Team building   At the event, each member of the team will be given the opportunity to make their statements to each member of the team in turn.

When statements are made to you by your colleagues give simple responses to each statement:

- yes
- no
- let me consider that.

The exchange of these statements will be made in accordance with the ground rules of feedback that will be explained by the trainers at the event. Apart from supervising this activity the role of the trainers will be to police all the ground rules. The purpose of this policing is to ensure that the event is both productive and positive.

Figure 6.3   *Team building brief*

On talking this briefing through, the invariable question asked of the trainer is, 'To what extent are people honest?', to which the only reply is 'As honest as you want to be.'

It is advisable for the trainer to give some thought to whom will be best suited, in their judgement, to begin this activity at the event. In making this choice the important criteria are:

- an individual able to offer both positive and negative requests of colleagues
- an individual who, through position or personality, has a wide pattern of contact with colleagues
- an individual not caught up in a major conflict or carrying a burden of unfinished business.

It is apparent that the first person to speak sets the climate for the rest of the exercise, so it is not worth leaving this element to chance. At the interview stage, I will ask the person I consider to be the best choice if they would be willing to take on this responsibility. At the start of the exercise on the event, I will explain both my criteria and reasons for choosing a particular person to the team.

Obviously, the trainer *can* make a bad choice, though the probability of making a good one is high.

Design features

As mentioned earlier in this chapter, the main design feature of these kinds of programmes is to start at the level of maximum risk. The reason for flouting the orthodoxy of normal interpersonal skills programmes (low to high risk, always) is that the team *knows* what issues have to be dealt with and, consequently, approach the event with a particular ambivalence. Part of this ambivalence is a *desire* to resolve the problems, while the other side is an *anxiety* about having to deal with the difficult situations. At the start of most events—if the recommendation for going ahead is a good one—this ambivalence is nicely poised on the edge. By starting at the level of highest risk—which the preparatory work clearly indicates—the team is very conscious of calculating, and having individual responsibility for, the level of risk. They are able, as it were, to lower themselves into the bath water bit by bit in response to the temperature of the water. If the trainer chooses to defer the moment of highest risk, then the team are likely to experience a mélange of feelings—including impatience, frustration and an increasing uncertainty—that is akin to suddenly leaping into the water without any clear idea of what to expect.

The second design feature—and the main reason for choosing this approach—is that the programme addresses first individual needs, then group process, because the team is unable to deal effectively with the task. What this means in practice, is that the *particular* always precedes the *general*, e.g., the team has to sort out the resistance of member X before the wider issue of dealing with resistance to organizational change can be raised. By working through these smaller issues, the teams do develop some practical ideas and strategies for how the wider issues may be tackled.

The intention is to work through both levels of process by the end of the second day, at the latest, so that there is time to take the necessary decisions about the team and, where appropriate, at the strategic level.

Under no circumstances does it make sense to deal with anything other than real issues. Substitute tasks are, therefore, totally inappropriate.

The ground rules   The aim of the introductory activities, like that of the preparatory work, is as much concerned with managing the process as it is with providing information about the event. Apart from meeting the obvious needs of providing guidance and structure, the process aims are, first, for the trainer to establish a role that makes it clear that they can provide protection to all concerned and, second, for the group to receive permission that to express feelings is legitimate. (This is a permission only—it is neither mandatory, nor, necessarily, to be achieved by one and all. The expression of feelings is not meant to be a benchmark of effectiveness for the event, the team or the trainer!)

The introductions themselves can, and should, be as simple as possible. Each person is asked to respond to two questions:

- What thoughts have you had about the event since the interviews?
- What feelings are you experiencing at the moment?

Typically, the latter question will reveal the level of anxieties and concerns. In listening to the team members, it is important that the trainer does not attempt to offer reassurances, e.g., 'Don't worry, I've run a lot of these events and no one has ever . . . (stormed off, refused to take part, been deeply mortified, etc., etc.)'. Instead, a better choice is to publicly acknowledge the reality of the concern, e.g., 'So you are concerned that you will not be able to cope with the negative feedback'. Another valuable response is to ask the person whether or not they want to take some explicit safeguards against the possibility of their fear being realized, e.g., 'Should you find that you are unable to cope with the negative feedback, what would you like to happen?' Any suggestions would obviously be added to the ground rules, e.g., 'It's OK to say that you do not want any more feedback'.

The way that the trainer responds in these early stages will have a major impact on the initial climate. If team members experience the trainer as *listening* and having no desire to *restrict* their choices (e.g., 'It's OK to be anxious *and* it's also OK not to be anxious'), then the content of what they say is unimportant. If, however, they start picking up non-verbal clues that the trainer is not managing their own feelings—either by attempting to suppress them or finding it difficult to keep them under control—then these early exchanges will lead to a heightening of emotions for all.

As part of the introductions, the trainer should offer their own thoughts and feelings to the team. By being last in the circle, this provides an opportunity to bridge into a brief outline of the structure. This structure has three elements:

1 for the team to review how it is currently operating by:

  • 'Do more of . . . Do less of . . . Continue doing . . .' exercise
  • the identification of team issues

2 Providing theory on matters raised in the above activities, e.g., effective teams, team dynamics, patterns of individual and group behaviour.
3 The team reaching decisions about its future operation by:

  • individuals setting their own action plans in response to feedback received
  • making decisions about the team issues.

The ground rules logged on a flipchart should include the following:

• confidentiality (see p. 13).
• the aims of the event are:

  —to improve the overall effectiveness of the team
  —to provide each member with the opportunity to say what they
    want and to ensure that they receive a clear response
  —for the team to review the management culture of the organization
    as well as the team
• the role of the trainer is to:

  —provide structure, guidance and theory
  —monitor and intervene regarding *how* you talk to each other rather
    than the *content* of what you say
  —offer feedback to individuals and the team
  —share responsibility for policing the ground rules
• the rules regarding feedback are:

  —for the *giver* to: be direct—talk to and look at the person
    be specific about the behaviour concerned
    see feedback as the *start* of a conversation, not the *end*
  —for the *receiver* to: ask for clarification where necessary
    think about what they say—beware of automatically accepting or
    rejecting
    check with others if feedback is a surprise
    not explain, justify or defend
    let the giver know what you are doing with the feedback
    limit your responses to accepting (in whole or part), rejecting or
    thinking about.

The concerns raised in the introductions may have led the team to formulate some additional ground rules that can be added to this list.

The exercises and theory

Individual behaviours

In view of the risk level, it is advisable that the trainer adopts a directive and controlling approach (see Interventions by the trainer later in this chapter). Therefore, there is little scope for deviation from the structure and the ground rules for each of the two major elements—the individual needs and the team issues. Any deviation from the structure, particularly in the early stages, will undermine the important need for protection. Such deviations will also make it difficult for the team to achieve some sense of completion. The one element of the programme where choice is both necessary and possible concerns the use of theory. What follows, therefore, is a detailed outline of how such an event can be managed.

Having set the ground rules and put them on display for the whole group to see, it is recommended that a brief theoretical scene-setting is provided. This would involve a brief description of the Schein model of an effective team (see p. 34, ff.) and, an outline of process symptoms (see p. 36-7). The rationale being offered is that the structure of the event involves, first, dealing with the individual needs and, second, then addressing the group process. By working in this sequence, the assumption is that it will be easier for the team to address the task concerns. In outlining this sequence, the intention is to provide a map for the trainer's direction, not to provide a discussion point for the team. If the team is senior or is charged with managing change in the organization, it is worth the trainer making explicit the link that team building is primarily concerned with achieving specific attitudinal and behavioural changes (see Figure 1.1, p. 5) that are central to the culture of the organization. Part of this linking is to ask them to pay attention to what happens over the next three or four days, not only at a personal but also at a strategic level, i.e., *my* feelings and responses are likely to be a guide to what *others* are likely to experience.

Making this cultural connection and scene-setting for the team should be completed within 30 minutes and the team should then be ready to move on to the exercise they have been asked to prepare at interview.

**Do more of . . .,
do less of . . .,
continue doing . . .**

Briefing

> In a minute I am going to ask X to start the exercise. They will choose the order in which to address members of the team and it is important that they do not rush the activity. When you are addressed, listen carefully to all the requests and feedback and, where necessary, ask for clarification. Once you understand, make a clear response on what you are doing with the feedback. No other person is allowed to comment or contribute to the exchange. At different points, I may check with X to see if they are OK. Equally, I may intervene with the receiver. Over to you, X.

Notes

During the exchanges, it is preferable for the trainer not to intervene, only doing so if there is a problem between the two people concerned or when the ground rules are clearly being flouted. The rule that causes most problem is the one of not defending, justifying or explaining behaviour. Unless there is obvious discounting of the feedback, the exchange of some explanation is advisable.

While the exchanges are proceeding, the trainer can usefully concentrate on two areas. First, the way the giver offers feedback. Second, the non-verbal behaviours of the receiver.

In the case of the former, some particular patterns that are likely to occur for the giver are shown in Figure 6.4.

- Being self-deprecating or minimizing their request, e.g., 'This is not really important, but . . .' or 'If you would be willing to do this for me, I would be terribly grateful'.
- Finding it difficult to be personal or direct, e.g., 'Other people have said these kinds of things about you' or 'It is generally understood that we should all behave in this way'.
- Finding it difficult to come to the point, e.g., 'What I am trying to say is . . .' or 'In addition, I would like to say'.
- Overelaborating, e.g., 'When you do this, it has the effect of, not only upsetting me, but making me think that I should be talking to someone else about the problem . . .'.
- Self-interrupting, e.g., 'And another thing . . ., which reminds me that I should have said . . . and, by the way . . .'.
- Trying very hard, e.g., 'Now, how can I put this . . . I wouldn't really say that, but, on the other hand, it is *nearly* right'.

- Denying their own feelings in the situation, e.g., 'I thought this feed-back might be of interest to you' (the speaker's agitation is not acknowledged).
- Reading a charge sheet, e.g., 'First, you should . . . Second, I want you to . . .

Figure 6.4   *Patterns of giving feedback*

When a pattern emerges, the trainer can intervene with the giver to draw this to their attention and to invite them to experiment with a more direct style.

The second area the trainer should pay attention to is the non-verbal behaviour of the receiver. Some particular patterns of behaviour (i.e., behaviours that are repeated many times) worth drawing to the attention of the receiver include those listed in Figure 6.5.

- Furrowed forehead, knitted brows, general tightness in the musculature.
- Physical agitation, e.g., drumming fingers and tapping feet; squirming in the chair.
- Difficulties in making normal eye contact, there being instead either avoidance or intense staring.
- Noticeable change in the pattern of breathing—light, rapid breathing or deep, slow and laboured breathing.
- Physical stroking of the arms, face and neck.
- Scratching, gouging and pinching.
- Complete blocking of any facial or other body signals so that it is difficult to pick up any clues as to how they are responding.

Figure 6.5   *Non-verbal patterns of behaviour exhibited by the receiver*

The purpose of drawing these observations to the attention of the receiver may be simply to increase their level of self-awareness. An equally important reason is to intervene before the person becomes overwhelmed by an internal process of thinking and/or feeling. The person may have spent some time brooding on a comment that appeared totally innocuous at the time. Without the intervention of the trainer, this internal process may reach a dramatic outcome, e.g., the person storming off, crying or challenging what is being said. This eventuality can arise when the person is not even involved in the action—their response can stem from an interaction between two other members of the team (for an explanation of what is happening, see the Drama Triangle section later in this chapter).

When X has completed the round, they are then asked to give themselves feedback using the same format, i.e., 'What I could do more of . . . less of . . ., continue doing . . . as a member of this team'. At this stage, they will be asked if there are any additional team issues that could be added to the list for later discussion (a number of these will emerge and are listed by the trainer during the individual exchanges in the feedback exercise). When these have been added, the trainer then offers feedback to X. The basis used for offering the feedback is the experience gained during the analysis and diagnosis as well as the event. The purposes of offering this feedback are two-fold. First, the trainer can offer feedback from a position of detachment, and is more liable to pick up the kind of individual behaviour patterns listed above. Second, to absent themselves from an activity demanded of others can be a cause of considerable resentment on the part of the team members. It also provides an opportunity for team members to deflect their discomfort by attacking the trainer.

As a general guide to the order in which team members may undertake the activity, the following points are relevant for most teams. First, it makes sense to place the leader at the midway point, with a view to trying to minimize their impact on the team. If the leader goes first, there is a danger that what follows is seen to be anticlimatic. If the leader goes last, there is a danger that their feedback is seen to be more authoritative than that of other members. On the same basis, if there are different levels of hierarchy in the group, these also need to be spaced out. If there is some particular advantage to be gained from the leader going first, e.g., this will free the team up to be more open, then it is obviously worth considering.

Second, rather than work with a preplanned sequence, the trainer would be advised to use their judgement about the appropriateness of individuals having their turn. The ways in which individuals are responding—both verbally and non-verbally—to the feedback of others should provide sufficient clues about their readiness. Third, the trainer would be advised to leave to the end those individuals who are obviously defensive, cynical or still toying with the size of the aperture of their 'open' mind. Usually, the accumulating evidence of safety and learning provided by their colleagues helps them to find their own level of security within the team. By contrast, it is often damaging to invite them to go early. Their unresolved anxiety and defensiveness can precipitate a major crisis within the team. For example, colleagues may attempt to defend them by attacking the trainer again, (see the Drama Triangle section later in this chapter).

The time this activity will take to complete is difficult to estimate because it is dependent on the level of unfinished business in the team. For a group of 12, it can take between 6 to 12 hours of class time. The information gathered in the analysis stage will provide a strong clue. When making estimates of the time required, it is advisable to be generous rather than tight as trying to achieve movement with one 'personality clash' can easily take over an hour.

When everyone has completed their feedback, the next task is the Individual Learning Review.

Individual Learning Review

Briefing

Individually, reflect on the requests made of you and the feedback that you have received. Then write down on a piece of paper:

- what you intend to do—be as specific as possible, e.g., 'At my next meeting with Y, I will summarize what she has said before I offer my view'
- in the light of what you know about yourself, how might you sabotage this plan, e.g., 'By wanting to achieve a result'
- what support could another member of the team provide to help you overcome that problem, e.g., 'By giving me feedback about the non-verbal clues of my impatience'?

Notes

When everyone has written down their answers, the trainer then asks one member of the team to take responsibility for collecting all these statements and having a collated list typed and circulated to all their colleagues. When this procedure has been followed, the outcomes are significantly higher than those times when the plans go no further than verbal intentions.

During the event the trainer is paying attention to the behaviour pattern of individuals and, it is only through descriptions that he or she hears about patterns of group process. Obviously, for the duration of this exercise, the trainer has suspended the 'normal' group process, apart from odd episodes that intrude. In addition to offering feedback to individuals on what they have noticed, the trainer ought to be anticipating what theory to offer as part of the second element of the programme. At the group process level, inputs on stages of group development (see p. 38, ff.) and individual needs in groups (see Figure 3.4, p. 37) provide useful bridging links to the team issues. Some useful theory about individual behaviour patterns can be provided by inputs on drivers, the Drama Triangle and confidence levels.

Drivers

The concepts of both drivers and drama triangles are drawn from Transactional Analysis.[1] They are both concerned with describing regular and recognizable patterns of behaviour that are essentially non-functional, i.e., the behaviours do not satisfy the underlying need, in fact, they are self-defeating. The drivers are behaviours and attitudes learned in the first few years of life and in relationship to parents. What underpins each driver—and there are five key ones in our culture—is a demand from the parent that the way to both please them, and to survive in the world, it is necessary to always satisfy one or more of the requirements given in Figure 6.6.

- *Be perfect* to set oneself the task of doing a perfect job, in spite of the fact that perfection is unobtainable.
- *Please me* to undertake responsibility for pleasing other people and always putting their needs before your own.
- *Try hard* based on the repeated injunction 'Needs to try harder', the process of trying is more important than that of achieving.
- *Hurry up* there is so much to do, and so little time available, hence the need to move at speed.
- *Be strong* as the world is a cold, hard place, only the strong will survive, while the weak will go to the wall. Any sign of vulnerability or expression of emotion is a hostage to fortune.

Figure 6.6 Drivers

Having swallowed these attitudes and learned the behaviours, we are each likely to switch on our favourite drivers when we feel under pressure. The commonality with all the drivers is that, initially at least, they are powerful motivators, but at some stage, the person will hit a point of failure brought on by a feeling of frustration, exhaustion, depression, impatience or anger and the person will dramatically switch off. For example, the Be perfect becomes a slob, the Hurry up collapses, the Please me becomes angry with others. This failure is then followed by feelings of guilt and remorse, plus a replay in the head of the command they were following. These experiences and feelings reinforce the need to Be perfect, Hurry up, etc.

These driver behaviours are often endorsed, explicitly or implicitly, by the organizations for which we work. A team, in managing one of its key boundaries, can reward a particular driver. For example, a team may only enter into conflict if the Please me boundary is threatened by the trainer. For such a team, conflict is avoided publicly, apart from the odd rare explosion, and only emerges in safe, third-party assassinations!

Having offered the theory, the trainer can invite the team to identify how, individually and collectively, these patterns affect their performance.

Drama Triangle   In a similar vein, according to Transactional Analysis we also develop an appetite for engaging in certain dramatic encounters, whether on a one-to-one basis or in groups. All that is required to do so is:

- a minimum of two people, though more provides greater variety of scenarios

- one of the people involved to either put themselves down in some way, e.g., 'I can't cope!', 'I'm useless', or to put the other person down, e.g., 'The trouble with you is . . .' or 'Poor old Joe, he needs my help'.

This provides the basic dynamics for the Drama Triangle (so called because it provides the basis for all drama). The triangle contains three roles, shown in Figure 6.7.

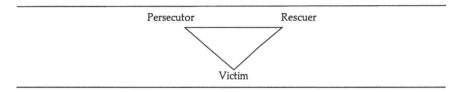

Figure 6.7   Drama Triangle

The roles are scripted as follows:

- *Persecutor* 'I am better than you; you are inferior. Because of this inequality I have the right to persecute you.' This persecution may be direct (physically or verbally) or through a third party, e.g., 'I would not put up with that if I were you.'
- *Rescuer* 'I know more than you; you are inadequate.' The rescuer identifies who needs help, when and by whom. An invitation is not required. A rejection of their services could leave them upset, e.g., 'I was only trying to help'.
- *Victim* 'I am helpless; others can manage.' The statements may be plaintive, 'I can't cope', weary, 'Why does this always happen to me', or stoical, 'Life is full of suffering'.

To illustrate how this works, I will analyse a situation described above—asking for volunteers for the feedback exercise.

The trainer asks for a volunteer to go next in the role negotiation exercise. Jack offers, but says, 'I don't think that I will do a very good job, but I will soon get it over with' (Victim). Jack starts giving feedback, quickly makes a 'mistake', looks distressed and apologizes to the team. Another member of the team, Dennis, says to himself, 'Poor old Jim' (Rescuer), and then tells the trainer, 'This is a stupid exercise, I told you people couldn't cope' (Persecutor). The trainer then starts defending the exercise (Victim) and Joe and Mary respond by agreeing with Dennis (Rescuer). At this point, Sarah enters and tells the rest 'To stop sabotaging the exercise' (Persecutor). The trainer then either continues with the exercise (and all this process goes underground to reappear later) or seeks to unravel the process.

The characteristics of the Drama Triangle are:

- roles are exchanged between individuals, often with each statement

- events move very quickly
- people end up with bad feelings
- in a team, it can paralyse any attempt at problem solving.

The underlying premise of the Drama Triangle is that each of us have a preference for one of the roles and are very skilled at finding the right people to engage with. The frequency and degree of our involvement in this process will vary. The majority of people will become involved infrequently, but others could approach many of their relationships in this dramatic fashion.

Having introduced this concept, the trainer can encourage team members to share their experiences, generally or as team members, of being involved in the process. A common knowledge of this concept provides an important preventative mechanism against future occurrences.

Self-confidence   Another important issue that often emerges through the normal process of self-disclosure and feedback is that of lack of confidence. In my experiences of running these events, one of the key turning points for the team is an open admission by a member that he or she lacks confidence. Such confessions are comparable to watching a dam being breached—within minutes, similar admissions are emerging all over the room. A lot of the behaviour that has hampered team effectiveness (including both driver and Drama Triangle behaviours) is being correctly described as ineffective fronts for vulnerability.

Therefore, a useful intervention may be to offer stroke theory (see p. 76–7), as a precursor to inviting team members to experiment with not only giving each other positive strokes, but, more importantly, giving them to themselves.

The other option is to invite the group to brainstorm a list of behaviours that can actively help them to develop self-confidence. Such a list might include the items in Figure 6.8.

- Give yourself positive strokes and enjoy them.
- Accept positive strokes from others.
- Respect your feelings and needs as being natural.
- Give yourself appropriate permissions—to be imperfect, please yourself, take your time, be weak and not to push yourself.
- Actively ask for support.
- Remember previous successes.
- Recognize that you can learn from mistakes without feeling bad.
- You have the freedom not to rescue, persecute or be a victim.

Figure 6.8   Positive self-influence

Having offered the theory, and time for reflection, the team should be ready to move away from individual process and begin to address the group process and task items contained in the team issues. At this stage in the programme, the trainer should make a dramatic step backwards to provide the team with maximum opportunity to implement their personal experiments.

Team issues

Briefing

> This group has two hours to discuss the issues allocated. For each issue, the group has to agree on a proposal for action. Each proposal must be resource neutral, must indicate who is responsible and give a date for completion. The group must record all proposals on a flipchart and be in a position to present their proposals to the team by the agreed time.

Notes

For this task the team are split into two groups, at random, and each has to elect a chairperson. The team issues that have accumulated are also randomly divided, with half the items being given to each group. The team leader is nominated as a resource to both teams and moves between the two teams as and when they want to. The purpose of this rule is to clearly pass over to the team freedom and responsibility to work on the issues that they have identified. This reverses the normal pattern of most team meetings and is often anticipated by the leader as a time for maximum discomfort. Invariably, they are pleasantly surprised by positive rather than negative proposals.

Unless really exceptional circumstances arise, it is unwise to extend the time limits. One of the common patterns that teams develop to avoid decision making is a strong belief that serious issues require a long time for discussion. Like many other beliefs, this is worth challenging. Therefore, the team is brought together to hear the presentations. The ground rules for these are that:

- each group presents their proposal(s) on an issue
- the receiving group can ask for clarification
- once the proposal(s) is understood the receiving group is limited to responding with the options of agreeing, offering a counterproposal or deferring it for further discussion.

In the event of a counterproposal, the original group are also constrained to the limitations on responses above. The team leader is always part of the receiving group and also has to operate according to these rules. As each item is worked through, the appropriate decision is recorded on a flipchart. This document becomes the second part of the action plan.

Action planning and review

The format and timing for the action planning having already been determined via the Individual Learning Review exercise and the decisions made during the Team Issues exercise, so there is no need to allocate additional time on the programme for this.

In addition to the follow-up with the trainer, most teams, in my experience, agree to review these plans periodically as part of their normal cycle of meetings. Invariably, this agreement is made in response to a team issue about the need to continue the process of team building.

The review meeting with the trainer should be held off-site, and will take a whole day. An interval of six months provides enough time for serious work to be carried out on the individual action plans. The major problem encountered on these review days is the integration of new members. In a period of six months, it is likely that the membership of a team will change. Most teams will have addressed this possibility on the original event. They will have taken some action to integrate the newcomer, but, unless that person has been through a comparable experience, they will only be able to appreciate the content outcomes. The process that led to these outcomes, and the individual behavioural experiments, are less likely to be understood. To ease the newcomer into the process side of team building—without putting them under inordinate pressure—the following format has been successfully used. First, each of the original members are asked to report on their Individual Learning Reviews. Second, the newcomer is invited to offer their observations on what they have noticed about the team. Third, they are then invited to make general or specific requests of team members. Fourth, and finally, the rest of the team are invited to offer feedback and/or requests to the newcomer.

Interventions by the trainer

To manage this kind of event, the trainer needs to be both directive and controlling when running the different elements, particularly in the patrolling of the ground rules. The nature of the direction and control is *not* related so much to what individuals or teams need to learn, but to their *methodology* of learning.

This need for directiveness can create problems for trainers who have assiduously developed a non-directive style. The whole notion of controlling a learning event can conflict with what they may espouse as important values to do with learning. However, the drawback of this traditional style is that it fails to provide team members with any sense of safety. The missing element has been defined as the 'three Ps':[2]

- *Protection* Being able to protect individuals from exceeding their personal level of risk and/or helping to retrieve them should this occur.
- *Permission* Empowering people to take the risk of breaking out of self-defeating patterns of behaviour, e.g., 'It's OK to be imperfect'.
- *Potency* The perceived ability to be able to cope with uncertainty and the credibility to be able to offer both protection *and* permission.

The general currency of interventions is still 'there and then', e.g., 'I noticed that you were smiling as he gave you the feedback. What were you thinking?' However, the focus of the 'there and then' is usually on the immediate past, i.e., two minutes to two days, so there are fewer escape holes for individuals. By talking about my behaviour—which you all witnessed—20 minutes ago, it is much harder for me to rationalize, deflect or avoid. When I talk about an event that happened back at work, weeks ago, that only involved one other member of the team, so I can successfully offer many imaginative versions.

Occasionally, and in response to problems rather than as a design feature, the trainer may intervene at the level of 'here and now'. Some reasons for this, and how to manage them, are given below.

One important feature of the trainer role is the need to shift dramatically, from being highly interventionist at the start to making minimum contributions in the later stages. The best way to effect this change for all concerned is to indicate right at the start that this will occur. During the small group work on the Team Issues exercise, the trainer can come and go in the session without saying a word. If the first part of the programme has been successful, this should not pose a problem.

It also provides an opportunity for the trainers and the clients to share perceptions, offer feedback and check out levels of satisfaction with the event.

Problems and how to handle them

Although the initial focus is on the relationships between individual members of the team, one of the key learning aims is the development of self-awareness. In addition to dealing with the immediate concerns of how X can improve her relationship with Y, it is intended that, by doing so, both X and Y have an improved understanding of the patterns of behaviours that they use in groups with others. This level of learning is, or should be, transferable to a whole number of situations.

The consequence of the personal learning approach is that, once begun, it can lead in many directions—not all of them intended or necessarily desirable. Because the aim is to examine unproductive patterns of behaviour as they impinge on the effectiveness of this team, the individuals will have developed and used the same patterns in a whole variety of contexts, from childhood onwards and this can give rise to two major problems. One could be the emergence for an individual of a powerful episode of unfinished business from a non-work context, e.g., in offering feedback to the team leader, a person begins to re-experience (not remember) an event, say, in their relationship with their father. The second possibility is that, under a similar kind of stimulus, a person is suddenly overwhelmed with feelings that bear no relationship to what is actually happening. The fact that similar experiences could be tripped by a whole range of stimuli—watching a film, having an argument, introspecting, listening to music, etc.—does not excuse the trainer from taking some responsibility for managing the consequences.

In my experience, such happenings do not occur by chance or appear from nowhere—a lot of clues are available if the trainer pays attention. First, there is the whole range of non-verbal behaviours (see Figure 6.5, p. 91 for some examples). Second, the person will display a verbal intensity, e.g., talking very fast or at length or being unwilling to let go of a point. The use of here and now interventions, e.g., 'What are you doing?' or 'What do you want?', are not designed to invite the person to explore the unfinished business. Instead, they are intended to draw the person's attention to their level of self-support, e.g., to breathe properly, to take their time, to regain control of their choices instead of allowing themselves to be overtaken by their feelings. Additionally, encouraging the person to actively exercise a choice now, 'What would you like to do—have a break, a cup of tea, time on your own?', is also purposeful. A trainer would be ill-advised to either say 'How do you feel?' or 'Tell me what is happening' in such a situation. If the person were to answer these questions at such a time, the trainer would move into a therapeutic relationship, which is outside the contract of the event.

The other major problem with this approach is the emergence of an intractable conflict between two members of the team. The two people have exchanged feedback and neither is willing to move towards repair. When this has become apparent, a useful choice for the trainer is to say 'It is apparent to me, at least, that neither of you are ready to move. As your relationship affects other team members, I would like to invite them to offer you suggestions on how you can find some way forward.' If this proves to be unproductive, then the next option is to request other members of the team to offer their ideas on how this problem can be managed at work. For example, another member of the team will offer their services as a facilitator to both parties to help them reach a basic agreement. Finally, the team—and it is important that it is the team rather than the leader—make demands that the two parties will meet minimum requirements for a working relationship.

Summary

In this chapter I have identified factors that suggest using the individual approach to team building. I have also described the key features of this approach and have offered a detailed structure, including the most relevant theory inputs, of how such a programme can be run. Finally, I have examined some of the issues that may face the trainer when using this approach. In the final chapter I will look at some of the wider implications of introducing team building in an organization.

References

1 Hay, Julia, *TA for Trainers*. McGraw-Hill, 1992. (For a full description of drivers, Drama Triangle and strokes.)
2 Crossman, P., 'Permission and protection', *TA Bulletin*, **5**, 19, 1963, pp. 152–3.

7 The organizational context

Introduction

In this final chapter, I wish to address some of the organizational issues that will affect the internal trainer's ability to deliver an event and the team's ability to continue the learning process after it. First, I wish to offer some general guidelines for the trainer on the use of the generic approaches detailed in the last three chapters. Second, I wish to offer some guidelines on how the process of learning and change can be continued with the trainer or through use of their own resources by the team. Third, I wish to look at some choices for developing the internal trainer. Finally, I would like to offer some ideas on how team building can be seen as a vehicle for changing the culture of an organization.

Use of the approaches

In the previous three chapters, I have written at some length about what I have chosen to describe as three generic approaches to team building (the use of the term 'generic' is an attempt to distinguish them from the kinds of approaches, associated with the work of individuals such as Adair, Belbin, etc.). I have also attempted to explain that each of the generic approaches is distinguished not by a view of what is an effective team, but by clear differences in learning objectives, methodology, trainer role and style and risk levels. This desire for separation is not the result of the pursuit of a theoretical model *per se*, but due to the fact that real problems arise when attempts are made to run programmes that cross these boundaries. In every case, such boundary crossing is to the detriment of the learning event, the team and/or the trainer. At the lowest level of risk, the problem will be one of confusion. To avoid this, and worse problems, I would recommend that trainers, particularly those who are new to team building, clearly centre a programme in one of these approaches. The trainer who is clear in their mind about the journey ahead is better able to provide basic safety for the team *en route*. It is conceivable that, over time, three different events could be provided for a particular team to match their pace of development. My experience, however, is that one appropriate intervention at the task, group or individual level should meet the development needs of any team for a good period of time.

Apart from the technical problems of mixing the approaches, or even worse, starting with one approach and 'ending up' in another, is that to do so is both ethically unsound and professionally incompetent. When the trainer undertakes the analysis and diagnosis with the client, this should lead to the formulation of a clear contract about the purposes and nature of the event. Having agreed the contract with the client, this should then be communicated clearly to the team. If the analysis and diagnosis is sound, then a task event, say, will both meet the learning aims *and* improve the effectiveness of the team. Events that start on this clear basis of agreement do not 'end up' becoming individual-based events because of a desire by the team. They do so because the trainer has selected activities, presented theories and made interventions, deliberately or through ignorance, that have influenced this direction. Apart from breaking the contract, such a mutation ensures that the original learning objectives cannot be achieved. For example, it is virtually impossible for a team to focus on the development of problem-solving skills when they are involved in a process of learning that requires the giving and receiving of personal feedback. The adoption of a different learning approach means that the contract cannot be fulfilled.

It is conceivable that the diagnosis for an event might prove faulty. For example, although the intention is to run a group event, it becomes apparent that a major obstacle to effectiveness is a lack of task skills. Should this occur, then the trainer and the client ought to renegotiate the contract with the team. This would involve giving the team sufficient information for them to make an informed judgement about the choices available. If the team make an informed choice, then the trainer is acting ethically and genuinely being flexible.

Although I will pick up the issue of trainer development and support later in this chapter, I want to say here that it should also be clear that the skill requirements for a trainer parallel the increase in risk associated with each approach. This means that a trainer new to team building would be well advised to work at the task level before considering an attempt at a group approach event. The trainer will then need experience at this level before being ready to attempt an individual approach event. Ideally, this skill development will be assisted by the opportunity to work with someone who has experience and skills in each area before the trainer goes solo. This cautionary note is being offered for the simple reason that it is the client and the team that has to live day by day with the consequences of professional incompetence.

Continuing the process

Following the team building event, the team and the consultant need to consider some consequential issues that may either help or hinder the process of learning and development. These issues are:

- debriefing
- follow-up activities
- interteam conflicts.

Debriefing   Any team will experience re-entry problems similar to those facing an individual returning from a management course.

The environment to which the team returns will have expectations, both positive and negative, about the outcomes of the event. In the case of staff working for the managers, these expectations may reflect a cynicism, i.e., the event is just a 'jolly' in a nice hotel or an unrealistic hope for a sudden improvement in the quality of their own working conditions. Where this latter improvement fails to materialize in the short term, staff then become cynical.

Other teams that have dealings with them often anticipate that the results of the event will present them with a problem. They sometimes believe that the returning team, having agreed some kind of game plan, will have learned skills that will enable them to win at their expense. Whether the expectations are as sharply defined as this or not, it is advisable that the returning team do consider—at the event—what their responsibilities are for communication to, and involvement in, the process of change.

If they anticipate a problem with another team, then the prospect of a joint activity may need to be considered (see Managing interteam issues below).

If individual members want to consider acting as facilitators to their own teams, then the trainer should take the opportunity to provide guidelines (see The manager as team builder below).

The publication of team plans to interested parties is a good point from which to start to deal with the possible range of expectations. This, however, needs to be followed by a face-to-face discussion and briefing about future plans for involvement in the process. When the team in question is the most senior in the organization and the intention is to take other teams through this process, it is highly advisable that members also have an opportunity to talk to their own teams about their personal experiences of the event. This off-the-record discussion, in which the person is able to talk about their fears and concerns about the event as well as offering a straight description of what occurred, does more to correct unrealistic expectations than any other kind of intervention.

Follow-up activities   In Chapters 4, 5 and 6, I described how the particular action plans readily provide the structure for a review session with the trainer. The aims of such sessions are:

- to review the level of learning and change that has occurred as a result of the event
- to identify those actions that have not been implemented and to identify the nature of the blockage

- to provide assistance to help the team deal with problems that have emerged subsequently.

In meeting these aims at the session, the team, within the agreed structure of reviewing the action plans, should take the major responsibility for the learning process. For this reason, the trainer should limit their own interventions to the asking of open questions, e.g., 'What happened?', 'How did you resolve the issue?' In addition, the team are likely to make specific requests of the trainer for assistance. In my experience, the common requests include:

- how to facilitate dealing with a conflict on a content issue or between individuals
- how to provide an opportunity for new members of the team to give and receive feedback in a safe environment
- how to provide theory inputs on issues affecting the team, e.g., the management of change, managing stress, etc.

Checking with the client some weeks before the event enables the trainer to receive early warning about such requirements and to be prepared on the day.

Managing interteam issues

One of the common problems identified in the course of a team building event is that of conflict with another team. This means that both teams expend a lot of time and effort in managing their external boundary (see p. 23). The nature of this 'management' may include:

- avoidance of contact
- blaming for perceived errors
- lack of cooperation
- even sabotage.

During the team building event, the trainer can help the team focus on its responsibilities for the conflict and identify strategies for improving the relationship. A more effective choice, however, is to see this activity as a precursor to a joint event with the other team. The origins of many of these interteam conflicts are often lost in folk memory, current members merely being involved in a continuation of the process of mistrust and selective perception. The intention of bringing both groups together is to unravel the growing tapestry of distrust jointly.

By taking the two teams off-site, the trainer can help them to address the problem of perceptions by means of the Intergroup Perceptions exercise.

Intergroup Perceptions

Briefing

> Consider the following three questions and record your answers on flipchart paper. Please be ready to present your answers in plenary session in 40 minutes.
>
> 1 What adjectives would you use to describe your team?
>
> 2 What adjectives would you use to describe the other team?
>
> 3 What adjectives would the other team use to describe your team?

Notes

Most teams, in my experience, begin to appreciate the underlying process as they start to answer the third question. During the presentations, both teams are usually ready to move away from the process of blaming and begin the next stage—problem solving.

A useful structure for achieving problem solving is the Intergroup Role Negotiation exercise.

Intergroup Role Negotiation

Briefing

> As a starting point for resolving the problems that exist, consider the following questions. Please record your answers on flipchart paper and be ready to present them to the other team in 45 minutes.
>
> 1 Specifically, in what ways can members of the other team help you do your job more effectively and with greater satisfaction?
>
> 2 Specifically, what changes can you and your colleagues make in your daily behaviour to assist the other team's effectiveness and satisfaction?
>
> 3 How might this team sabotage the proposals listed in your answer to question 2?

Notes

Ideally, both teams should have undertaken team building prior to this intervention but this may not always be the case. The success of this intergroup intervention is not dependent on prior team building, but on a tight control by the trainer in running these activities. Unless there are extenuating circumstances (e.g., size of teams, major personality conflicts, unresolved process issues within one of teams, etc.) a day should be sufficient for resolving these problems.

The manager as team builder

Although the best choice for team building, of whatever type would involve an external facilitator and accommodation away from the immediate workplace, these resources and facilities may not be available for every manager and their team.

Even when these resources *are* available, the manager might want to consider alternative approaches for other reasons. For example, the team or manager, might consider that there is already a sufficient level of openness and trust within the team, so they have the necessary resources to work with. Alternatively, the manager may feel that there is insufficient trust for an intensive event and that there is a need to proceed slowly. Therefore, a cautious first step is required.

When the manager decides to take on the role of team builder, there are two particular issues that need to guide their choice of action. These issues are:

- the role of the manager
- the level of risk.

The role of the manager

Whatever the nature of the relationship of the manager with the team—good, bad or indifferent—it will need to be redefined to allow them to take on the role of the facilitator. The manager will never be able to achieve the same advantages that should be enjoyed by an external facilitator, which are:

- not having a vested interest in the team's decisions
- offering a relationship of neutrality to all members of the team
- being unable to influence the future career path of an individual within the organization
- having an objectivity based on a wider experience of team process
- having knowledge and skills of individual and group process.

However, in taking on the role of facilitator, the manager will need to:

- define the objectives of the team building activity, e.g., develop skills, understanding, team spirit, etc.
- openly express their feelings and concerns about taking on the role
- facilitate open discussion and decision making
- offer their own views on issues as other members of the team
- clarify the decision-making process to be used by the team
- be objective and impartial with each team member
- clarify the parameters of discussion, i.e., what can be discussed and make it clearly understood that open discussion will *not* lead to negative consequences when individuals do speak their mind.

Many teams will respond to the prospect of team building with suspicion, hostility, apathy or fear. The manager taking on this difficult role must not be deflected by these responses and should continue with invitations to the team to change the climate.

The level of risk   As a general principle, the manager's approach should include small, low-risk activities as often as possible. For example, a good starting position is for the manager to ask, at the end of a normal meeting, for each member to express their level of satisfaction/dissatisfaction with the meeting. The sole reason for the request is to receive feedback. The next steps in order of increasing level of risk could involve:

- putting team building as an item for discussion on the agenda of the next meeting
- specifying a topic for discussion at a future meeting, e.g.:

  —What kind of team do we want to be?
  —What are the aims of the team?
  —How is this team effective/ineffective?
  —What factors help/hinder this team?
  —As a team we work best when . . . As a team we perform badly when . . .

- allocating the whole of a normal meeting to a discussion of team performance
- having one-on-one meetings with staff as a precursor to a day on team building
- going off-site for half or one day.

As the team progresses through this kind of sequence, it is very important that the team leader pays attention to the level of risk that the team will tolerate productively. For example, a level of anxiety is healthy and functional. Should this anxiety approach fear, then the activity will generate resistance rather than learning. The team will also need to have positive experiences of the manager in the facilitator role before they will readily increase the level of risk. Some additional guidelines for managing the risk level are, first, for the manager to ensure that discussion focuses on future action, not past events, and, second, for any form of blaming (self or others) to be avoided.

Under no circumstances should a manager attempt any approach to team building that includes the exchange of personal feedback. Instead, they should work at the task or group level. It is highly unlikely that a manager and a team have a sufficient level of support and the necessary skills to manage the feedback process at the individual level.

Developing the trainer

For many internal trainers, the move from the provision of interpersonal skills programmes to that of facilitating team building events can be a demanding one. Apart from having to deal with the technical and expertise demands of designing an event, the trainer is often faced with the need to redefine the nature of their role within the organization. For many trainers, this redefinition involves a move away from a service-driven approach to training, i.e., providing x number of skills and knowledge based programmes as agreed with managers, to a consultancy-based service that may involve the trainer saying 'No' to a client.

The ability to manage the political realities of saying 'No' to senior managers will be heavily constrained by the trainer's belief in themselves and skills of assertion. For many trainers this presents a catch-22 situation: without the experience and expertise of offering a consultancy service to clients, their level of belief in themselves is likely to be low, which will undermine their capacity to assertively influence senior managers. One way out of this situation is for the internal trainer to bring in an external consultant who has both the experience and the willingness to pass on their skills and knowledge. In this situation there are, thus, two levels of consultancy attending every event:

1 the internal trainer is the client to the external consultant
2 the team leader is client to the training team of internal trainer and external consultant.

In selecting the external consultant, the internal trainer (in the role of client) needs to have a very clear list of needs to be satisfied. Such a list should include those shown in Figure 7.1.

- The consultant actually runs team building events, as opposed to management skills and/or knowledge-based programmes run for teams. (Unfortunately, this is a common problem and, ironically, the internal trainer can often run a better quality event than the consultant.)
- The consultant undertakes some form of analysis and diagnosis before the event and the internal trainer is involved in these activities as an equal partner.
- The consultant does not ask for separate meetings with the client and the client system.
- The consultant genuinely has a choice of methodologies and approaches to use to meet the identified needs of the team.
- The consultant offers feedback and is also willing to respond to feedback from both the internal trainer and the client system.
- The consultancy team approach maximizes the strengths of both parties and the external consultant does not encourage any form of dependency.
- The materials used by the consultant can be used by the client at no additional charge.

Figure 7.1   Criteria for selecting an external consultant

Working within these criteria, most internal trainers should have the basic knowledge and expertise requirements for running task and group events with an external consultant. There is likely to be a deficiency of knowledge and experience, however, for individual-based events. The trainer wishing to develop in this area will need to consider attendance on external programmes as an adjunct to their personal development.

Once they have gained experience in this, by working with consultants and attending development programmes, internal trainers would be well advised to work in tandem on team building events. Apart from offering each other support before, during, and after, events, the partners should be able to safeguard each other against the potential loss of objectivity when working with a difficult team.

A facilitator's programme

One of the reasons for writing this book was to address a particular gap in the available literature, i.e., a need for a step-by-step guide to team building for the trainer. Unfortunately, at the time of publication, there is a similar gap in the provision of external training programmes to meet this need. A number of training organizations offer programmes that aim to assist trainers in becoming internal consultants, but they do not address the particular requirements facing team builders. There are obviously programmes in the 'brand name' approaches to team building (Adair, Belbin, etc.), but their major concern is to sell the model of team effectiveness associated with the brand name.

For large organizations that have a number of training personnel, it is possible to devise and provide a programme for facilitators to enable trainers to review and experiment with the generic approaches to team building given earlier. As an indication of how this might be structured, the following is a description of a programme that I run for trainers.

Day 1

12.30	Arrival and coffee
1.00	Lunch
2.00	*Introductory activities*

Introductions, nature of the programme, ground rules for learning [Particular ground rules relevant to the learning group are:

- you do not have to prove anything to yourself or to others
- it is OK to make mistakes
- anyone involved in competition with others will be asked to make the competition explicit, which will include the public awarding of marks for performance.]

2.30	*Team building*

Definition and nature of team building [Small groups are asked to agree a definition and identify characteristics that distinguish it from interpersonal skills training.]

3.30	Tea
3.45	*Facilitator skills*

Identification of skills [Small group exercise followed by plenary discussion.]

4.30   *The consultant relationship*
         [Theory input on the stages of consultancy described in
         Chapter 1 followed by a small group exercise, during which,
         each person acts as a consultant to a potential client.]

6.00   Close

Day 2   9.00   *Approaches to team building*
         Description of the generic approaches to team building
         [After the theory input, they are asked to assess, in small
         groups, the implications of each approach for facilitator
         and teams.]

10.30   Coffee

10.45   *Risk levels*
         The nature of risk and how it can be managed
         [In small groups, they are asked to ascertain the risk factors
         associated with each approach.]

1.00   Lunch

2.00   *Workshop 1*
         Participant-designed workshop in which each member of the
         group runs a team building activity or session.
         [Prior to the event, members are given access to the published
         resources listed on p. 116 to aid their choice. There is a clear
         expectation that, during the workshop, at least ten different
         activities will be run to cover the task, group and individual
         approaches. Each session is reviewed in terms of feedback to the
         trainer and the nature of the activity.]

6.00   Close

Day 3   9.00   *Learning blocks and resistances*
         Theory input and exercises
         [Based on the theory described on p. 25–7, the group are asked
         to identify their personal learning blocks and experiences of
         resistance.]

10.30   Coffee

10.45   Developing strategies to manage resistance in groups and
         individuals
         [Based on their earlier self-analysis, the groups are asked to
         brainstorm strategies for dealing with anticipated problems.]

1.00   Lunch

2.00   *Workshop 2*
         As Workshop 1

Day 4   9.00   *Organizational interventions*
         Cultural factors affecting team building
         [Small group exercise identifying cultural factors that help
         or hinder the approaches to team building.]

10.30	*The internal consultant*

Issues of credibility and authority
[Work in small groups and hold plenary sessions to identify ways in which to develop personal credibility.]

1.00	Lunch
2.00	*Workshop 3*

As Workshops 1 and 2

6.00	Close

Day 5 9.00 *Action planning*

Parallel small, group activities:

- debriefing with tutors
- action planning for the return to work

[The main purpose of the individual debriefing is to help each individual identify a development strategy, including both formal and informal opportunities.]

12.30	Review of programme
1.00	Close

The above programme is designed to accommodate ten delegates and is run by two tutors—an external consultant and an internal trainer. By the end of the week, all delegates have a clear idea and experience of the three generic approaches and are able to put their previous knowledge of the 'brand name' approaches into a wider context.

In addition to providing theory and an opportunity to identify and practise skills, the programme seeks to address a major problem of attitude among trainers. This problem is to help trainers move away from the belief that they need to be in control of the event from first contact with the client to the final review. Instead, they are encouraged to focus always on the needs of the client and the choices that they need to make during the process of change. In seeking to maintain this focus, the trainers are encouraged to prize common sense above theoretical knowledge. For example, addressing the simple question of whether or not the behaviour of a team is purposeful. When they are attempting to solve a problem do they succeed? If not, who or what is the problem?

During the course of five days, trainers on the programme do begin to recognise that the key to credibility as facilitators is to use the skills of seeing clearly and speaking plainly. Introspection and theoretical analysis are poor substitutes for these skills.

A strategy for team building

Throughout this book my approach to team building has been largely instrumental, i.e., seeking to describe what is involved in the process. In this final section, I would like to take a wider view that suggests that team building as a process provides a vehicle for changing the culture of an organization.

Teams do not exist in isolation, they are subsystems of the organizations. As such, their characteristics and qualities reflect and reinforce the wider culture. In the UK, until recently, teambuilding has been seen as either an option for remedial training, i.e., to help a team improve poor performance, or as a vehicle for developing a corporate spirit within an organization (hence the popularity of outdoor approaches). In the last few years, as a separate but parallel development, organizations have invested time and resources in the implementation of quality management initiatives that have sought to make fundamental changes in behaviours and attitudes as well as working practices. For many, this has involved the setting up of teams charged with a responsibility for innovating change. Unfortunately, after a short existence, these project teams are apt to decline and wither away, along with the procedures that they monitored. Like transplants, they are rejected by the host body. It seems to be a process repeated *ad nauseum* by organizations. The depressing debris of failed panaceas stretches endlessly over the years.

What the majority of these procedural-driven initiatives seek to rectify is either the absence of good working practices or the removal of unhelpful attitudes and behaviours. In terms of the organizational model developed by E.L. Trist,[1] it is to do with the problems identified in the informal social system (see Figure 7.2).

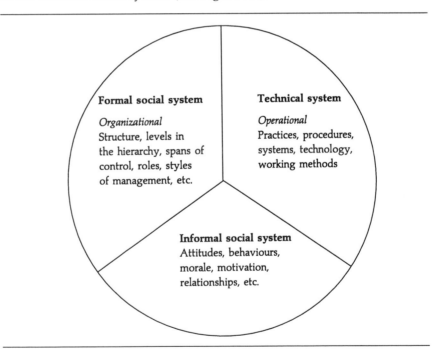

Figure 7.2 *The socio-technical system*

Although these three systems are highly interrelated, organizations seek to positively influence the informal social system by making changes in the other two areas, seeking to influence behaviours and attitudes by making changes in either the technical or formal systems. Invariably, these change strategies are top-down approaches, which just create further problems in the informal social system. The most common problem generated is that of increased resistance to further organizational change!

To develop an innovative and learning organization, the problem can be addressed more directly and the approach does not require the adoption of a philosophy or additional procedures based on major changes in the formal or technical systems. Only a few organizations appear to recognize that, by providing teams with an opportunity to undertake their own analysis and diagnosis through team building, there is a realistic chance of changing the culture. The introduction of alien procedures and ideas, however meritorious in intent, simply generate more systems and changes and—along with all the other technical and procedural changes that have to be accommodated—they will be discredited and disowned by members of the organization. Such changes are always imposed on the organization, never generated and driven from within. Team building, however, seeks to promote a process of renewal that reflects and develops from the history and culture of the organization. Such changes have the virtue of making sense to the people involved, so they are able to own them.

Such a strategy involves starting from the top with a view to working down through the organization, *but it does not involve the need to 'sheepdip' every team.* Team building, in this context, should be offered selectively and the approach used should be the one that addresses the behaviours and attitudes of individual members of the organization, i.e., the individual approach. One of the implicit aims of this approach is the empowerment of people at every level of the hierarchy.

This approach to team building is prescriptive in that it attempts to develop a style of management that is participative. The development of this style, however, is dependent on the ability of the event to assist individuals to be more assertive and proactive, both as members of particular teams and in their wider roles within the organization. It is also dependent on having a client at the top of the organization who is not only willing to encourage their staff to take the opportunities provided, *but who also has the ability to respond to feedback.* Such a response involves the client giving up power and responsibility and stepping into the uncertainty of team-driven management. This need is particularly important in organizations that have cultivated a more traditional style of leadership and are now discovering that large and complicated organizations are not amenable to change, no matter how charismatic or dynamic the person in charge. In fact, such leaders are often part of the problem rather than the solution, i.e., it is their ideas or solutions that have to be sold. The need for change is the challenge facing both public and private organizations. In my experience, the often-maligned public sector is actually moving further and faster in the right direction.

Summary   In this final chapter I have offered some guidelines on the use of the three generic approaches. I have also looked at some post-event problems that may need to be addressed, e.g., the debriefing on return, follow-up reviews and managing interteam conflicts. I have then offered some choices for the manager who wishes to act as facilitator to their team. In the wider organizational context, I have looked at some of the development issues facing the internal trainer. Finally, I have offered a view of team building as a vehicle for organizational change.

Reference   1 Trist, E.,L., 'The Socio-technical Perspective' in *Perspectives on Organization Design and Behaviour.* van de Ven, A., and Joyce, W.F., (eds) Wiley-Interscience, 1981.

Bibliography

Team building approaches

Adair, John, *Effective Teambuilding*. Gower, 1986.

Part I is concerned with a theoretical description of group and individual behaviour; Part II is concerned with building and maintaining high-performance teams.

Belbin, R.M., *Management Teams: Why They Succeed or Fail*. Heinemann, 1981.

Development of the team roles model.

Blake, Robert, Mouton, Jane and Allen, Robert, *Spectacular Teamwork: How to Develop the Leadership Skills for Success*. Sidgwick & Jackson, 1987.

The authors identify seven team cultures reflecting varying levels of excellence and illustrate them with a series of true-to-life studies.

Dyer, William G., *Team Building: Issues and Alternatives* (2nd ed.). Addison-Wesley, 1987.

Description of the development of team building as a concept. Chapters on diagnosis, planning the programme and dealing with particular kinds of teams, e.g., the complacent team.

Maddox, Robert, *Team Building: An Exercise in Leadership*. Kogan Page, 1988.

A manager's guide to team building through the development of appropriate leadership skills. Includes questionnaires to aid diagnosis.

Margerison, Charles and McCann, D., *Team Management*. Mercury, 1990.

Description of their team roles model. The roles are: Creato-innovators, Explorer-promoters, Assesor-developers, Thrusters-organizers, Concluder-producers, Controller-inspectors, Upholder-maintainers, Reporter-advisers.

Parker, Glenn M., *Team Players and Teamwork: The New Competitive Business Strategy*. Jossey-Bass, 1990.

Based on a model of four team roles: Contributor, Collaborator, Communicator and Challenger. Also looks at personal development as well as business growth within the team.

Woodcock, Mike and Francis, Dave, *Organization Development Through Team Building*. Gower, 1981.

The core of the text consists of some unique instruments designed to enable users to answer critical questions, e.g., is the team ready for building and does the organization need external help?

Team performance

Hastings, Colin, Bixby, Peter and Chaudhry-Lowton, Rani, *Superteams: A Blueprint for Organizational Success*. Fontana, 1986.

About teams that perform outstandingly well—the superteams. Based on the Ashridge teamworking approach, it examines the role and development of such teams.

Hicks, Robert F. and Bone, Diane, *Self-managing Teams*. Kogan Page, 1990.

Self-managing teams are small, autonomous work groups or business teams that contract with higher management to take complete responsibility for a product, project or service.

Katzenbach, Jon R. and Smith, Douglas K., Smith, *The Wisdom of Teams*. Harvard Business School Press, 1993.

Two senior McKinsey & Company consultants talked with hundreds of people to discover what differentiates various levels of team performance, where and how teams work best and how to enhance their effectiveness.

Fisher, Kimball, *Leading Self-directed Work Teams*. McGraw-Hill, 1993.

Examines the application of Self-directed Work Teams (SDWTs) and how they are replacing entrenched, autocratic, boss-driven organizations. Also profiles team leader practices and skills.

Source materials for activities

Adair, John, *et al.*, *A Handbook of Management Training Exercises*, 2 vols. British Association for Commercial and Industrial training (BACIE), 1980–2.

Volume I contains 25 exercises with background notes, while Volume II contains references to the background notes.

Brandes, Donna and Phillips, Howard, *Gamesters Handbook: 140 Games for Teachers and Group Leaders*. Hutchinson, 1978.

Exercises arranged in four sections: social development, personal development, concentrative (focusing), introductory.

Francis, Dave and Young, Don, *Improving Work Groups: A Practical Manual for Team Building*. University Associates, 1979.

Part I describes the theory of team building and group dynamics. Part II contains 46 exercises.

Johnson, David W. and Johnson, Frank P., *Joining Together: Group Theory and Group Skills*. Prentice-Hall, 1975.

Exercises arranged in sections—leadership, groups, etc., and includes short theory sections.

Jongeward, Dorothy and James, Muriel, *Winning with People: Group Exercises in TA*. Adison-Wesley, 1973.

Brief sections on theory with many individual and group exercises.

Pfeiffer, J. William, *The Encyclopedia of Team Building Activities*, 2 vols. San Diego: Pfeiffer & Company, 1991.

In each volume, the activities are grouped under subject headings, e.g., Team Effectiveness, Values, Feedback, Role Clarification, etc.

Pfeiffer, J. William and Jones, John E., *Annual Handbook for Group Facilitators*, 11 vols. University Associates, 1972–82.

Each annual volume contains structured experiences, lecturettes, learning instruments, resources, theory and practice papers.

Pfeiffer, J. William and Jones, John E., *A Handbook of Structured Experiences*, 10 vols. University Associates, 1974–83.

The 8 volumes contain 194 different training activities. As with their other titles, the publishers encourage trainers to reproduce the material for training and educational purposes.

Woodcock, Mike, *50 Activities for Teambuilding*. Gower, 1989.

Identifies the building blocks of effective teamwork (e.g., roles, objectives, support and trust, etc.) and indexes the relevance of the activities to these factors.

Woodcock, Mike, *Team Development Manual*. Gower, 1979.

Has introductory text on improving teamwork, then 45 activities and 9 lecturettes on group processes.

Individual and group behaviour

Berne, Eric, *What Do You Say After You Say 'Hello'?: The Psychology of Human Destiny*. Corgi, 1975.

Contains a chapter on the basic concepts of TA, but is primarily concerned with describing and analysing different 'life scripts', i.e., patterns of individual behaviour.

Bion, W.R., *Experiences in Groups: And Other Papers*. Tavistock Publications, 1968.

Description of the Tavistock approach to group training and the management of group dynamics.

Boshear, Walton C. and Albrecht, Karl G., *Understanding People: Models and Concepts*. University Associates, 1977.

Concise descriptions of models and concepts that aid understanding of the individual, pairs, groups and organizations.

Clark, Neil, *Managing Personal Learning and Change*. McGraw-Hill, 1990.

Examines the processes involved in personal learning and change and identifies the learning relationship needed to cope with learning blocks and resistances.

Clark, Neil, Phillips, Keri and Barker, Dave, *Unfinished Business: The Theory and Practice of Personal Process Work in Training*. Gower, 1984.

Having identified three approaches to learning, the authors describe and evaluate the tactical and strategic interventions that a trainer can use to aid learning.

Heron, John, *Dimensions of Facilitator Style*. Human Potential Research Project, University of Surrey, 1977.

Paper based on workshops run by Heron. Contains six-dimensional model of facilitator style.

Heron, John, *The Facilitators' Handbook*. Kogan Page, 1989.

Chapters on group dynamics and the development of facilitator styles.

Consultancy

de Board, Robert, *The Psychoanalysis of Organizations*. Tavistock Publications, Routledge, 1978.

Covers the contributions of Freud, Klein, Bion and Kurt Lewin to our understanding of individual, group and organizational processes.

Schein, Edgar, *Process Consultation*, (2nd ed.) 2 vols. Addison-Wesley, 1988.

Volume I outlines the basic concepts and techniques of process consultation, while volume II looks at applications of the model within organizations.

Walton, Richard E., *Confrontation and Third Party Consultation*. Addison-Wesley, 1969.

Primarily concerned with the management of interpersonal conflict as an organization development (OD) intervention.

Index